Hunter-gatherers

Hunter-gatherers

Hunter-gatherers

Mesopotamia

Uruk Susa

NEAN

Giza Ur Sumer

Harappa Yellow River Valley

qara Memphis Mehrgarh Mohenjo-Daro

Old Indus

Kingdom Valley

of Egypt

gatherers

INDIAN OCEAN

Hunter-gatherers

World Map c. 2500 BCE

Transition to agriculture

Agricultural areas

Urban areas

Urban hinterland

ANCIENT WORLD
IN YOUR POCKET

OVER 3,000 ESSENTIAL FACTS

General Editor:
PAUL BAHN

BARNES & NOBLE
NEW YORK

Designer: Ian Hunt

Acknowledgements
Paul Bahn and Elwin Street Productions would like to thank the the
contributing writers of this book:
Mesopotamia, Christopher Edens; Egypt, Joyce Tyldesley; South Asia,
Jane McIntosh; Far East, Margarete Pruech; Africa, Anne Solomon;
Bronze Age Aegean, David Gill; Europe, Peter Bogucki; Classical
Civilization, David Gill; Australia & Oceania, Caroline Bird; North America,
Philip Duke; Mesoamerica, Andrea Stone; South America, Jason Nesbitt.
Many thanks are also due to Victoria Leitch.

See page 144 for picture credits

ISBN-13: 978-0-7607-9409-8
ISBN-10: 0-7607-9409-X

10 9 8 7 6 5 4 3 2 1

Printed and bound in China by Midas Printing International Limited

Conceived and produced by
Elwin Street Limited
144 Liverpool Road
London N1 1LA
www.elwinstreet.com

Contents

MESOPOTAMIA

First civilizations

Mesopotamia, the land "between the rivers" Euphrates and Tigris, was home to one of the world's first civilizations. Mesopotamian civilization had taken form by 3500 BCE, and it endured for nearly four millennia. This area is divided into several distinctive regions. Southern Mesopotamia is the alluvial plain of Iraq, south of Baghdad, where the two rivers flow near each other before joining and emptying into the Persian Gulf. Northern Mesopotamia is the limestone plateau into which the two rivers are incised in northern Iraq and eastern Syria. In antiquity, as today, the region was home to a constantly changing mosaic of ethnicities and languages. Southern Mesopotamia was home to Sumerians, Akkadians, and Babylonians (among others), each of which gave their name to the area at different points in history. Assyrians were the best known inhabitants of Northern Mesopotamia, but their homeland was only a small area on the Tigris river.

Early farming villages

Mesopotamia's climate is dry. Rain-fed farming is possible (although often precarious) in parts of Northern Mesopotamia, but elsewhere in the region farming requires mastery of irrigation. The region

Timeline

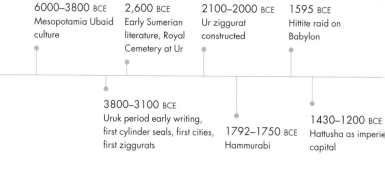

6000–3800 BCE
Mesopotamia Ubaid culture

2,600 BCE
Early Sumerian literature, Royal Cemetery at Ur

2100–2000 BCE
Ur ziggurat constructed

1595 BCE
Hittite raid on Babylon

3800–3100 BCE
Uruk period early writing, first cylinder seals, first cities, first ziggurats

1792–1750 BCE
Hammurabi

1430–1200 BCE
Hattusha as imperial capital

contains few natural resources (aside from petroleum), whereas the mountain belts east and north of Mesopotamia are rich in minerals and other resources. Yet by 6000 BCE Southern Mesopotamia hosted thriving agricultural villages that multiplied across the landscape over the next two millennia. These villages contained small temples and large communal structures, as well as family residences, and the roots of Mesopotamian civilization may be dimly perceived in them.

FACT
Before they created kingdoms during the tenth century BCE, the Aramaeans were wandering animal-herders much given to raiding settled peoples. During the eleventhth century their persistent raids caused great difficulties in Assyria and Babylonia.

Pastoralism

Animal-herding was an important economic activity across the Near East, providing wool and hides, milk and milk products, and meat. Pastoralism was usually integrated with agriculture: a family might farm and herd animals, or specialized groups might exchange agricultural and pastoralist products.

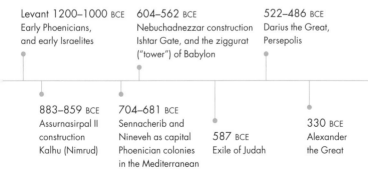

Levant 1200–1000 BCE
Early Phoenicians,
and early Israelites

604–562 BCE
Nebuchadnezzar construction
Ishtar Gate, and the ziggurat
("tower") of Babylon

522–486 BCE
Darius the Great,
Persepolis

883–859 BCE
Assurnasirpal II
construction
Kalhu (Nimrud)

704–681 BCE
Sennacherib and
Nineveh as capital
Phoenician colonies
in the Mediterranean

587 BCE
Exile of Judah

330 BCE
Alexander
the Great

Urban civilization

Shortly after 4000 BCE, the Ubaid culture underwent rapid changes; by 3500 BCE it had taken on the discernible features that would characterize Mesopotamian civilization until its disappearance less than 2000 years ago. It was an urban civilization, and by 3300 BCE the largest cities already held populations of 50,000 people; by 2800 BCE these had doubled in size. The urban centers lay on a network of major canals surrounding the two rivers, which supplied water for farming and domestic use and also served as transportation routes.

Impressions on clay

The cuneiform writing system began taking form around 3500 BCE, when bureaucrats in temples started impressing geometric shapes on clay to denote different quantities of commodities such as wheat and sheep. Gradually, new signs representing whole words, and then syllables, were added to the repertoire, and the signs themselves were stylized so that they could be written with a stylus. By 2600 BCE real literature was being produced, such as temple hymns, compilations of proverbs, and the self-praise of kings. The oldest cuneiform texts were composed in Sumerian.

BELOW Sumerian cunieform tablet, c. 3rd millenium BCE.

Civilization chart

South Mesopotamia Ubaid culture	c. 6000–3800 BCE
South Mesopotamia Uruk period	3800–3100 BCE
South Mesopotamia Early Dynastic city-states	2900–2330 BCE
Akkadian empire	2330–2200 BCE
Ur III state/empire	2100–2000 BCE
Old Babylonian dynasty	1894–1550 BCE
Canaanite civilization	2000–1200 BCE
Anatolia, Hittite New Kingdom	1430–1200 BCE
Levant	1200–1000 BCE
Neo-Hittite kingdoms	c. 1200–600 BCE
Aramaean kingdoms	c. 1000–600 BCE
United Israel	c. 1000–922 BCE
Samaria	922–722 BCE
Judah	922–587 BCE
Neo-Assyrian empire	934–612 BCE
South Arabian civilization	800 BCE–575 CE
Neo-Babylonian empire	612–539 BCE
Achaemenid Persian empire	559–330 BCE

FACT

The city of Ur, in the deep south of Mesopotamia, existed from prehistoric times until about 2,000 years ago. But the Chaldeans, with whom the Bible associates the city, appeared in Southern Mesopotamia only in the ninth century BCE, long after the time of Abraham.

Art

Early Mesopotamian art was extremely diverse, but much of it did focus on the intersection of religion and political authority. Stone statues of worshippers, either naked or dressed in the flounced skirt of the Sumerians, were dedicated at temples; small images of lion-headed eagles and human-headed bulls, representing divinities, were rendered in precious materials; limestone vases and plaques bore scenes of cultic rituals, victorious warfare, and other deeds of kings. The grave goods interred in the Royal Cemetery at Ur, dated to around 2600–2500 BCE, brilliantly illustrate the trappings of a Sumerian court. Among these objects are lyres and figurative art constructed of nacre, carnelian, and lapis lazuli inlaid over wood frames; and headdresses, helmets, and weapons of precious metal.

LEFT
Mesopotamian art; depiction of a bull on a Babylonian city wall.

Natural and abstract gods

Mesopotamian religion involved a pantheon of gods, many of which personified natural forces as well as more abstract qualities. Thus Shamash was the sun-god and the deity of justice; Ishtar was the goddess of fertility and of love. Each city contained many temples dedicated to the gods, but the main temple belonged to the patron god of that city. Over time the importance of a god might change with the political fortunes of a city. Marduk became the "national god" when Babylon emerged as the political center of the south; Assur was the eponymous supreme deity of the Assyrian empire.

Human sacrifice at Ur

Several of the tombs in the Royal Cemetery at Ur contained the skeletons of servants and of cattle yoked to carts, sacrificed to accompany their royal masters in death. The significance of human sacrifice in Sumeria is uncertain.

Temples and palaces

Temples were thought of as houses of gods. Some important temples were placed upon a ziggurat, an artificial mountain formed by superimposing square terraces, each smaller than the one below, with a ramped staircase ascending to the temple at the top. Although similar to early Egyptian pyramids in shape, ziggurats were religious rather than burial structures. Famous ziggurats include those at Ur (twenty- first century BCE) and Babylon (sixth century BCE.)

Palaces were the other focal point of public life. As well as the residence of the royal family, palaces were the work-place of the administrators, scribes, craftsmen, and other specialists in royal service. As a result, palaces incorporated numerous "divisions:" private residential suites for the royal family, an audience hall with ancillary offices for public business, administrative offices, and stores of food and drink, and the kingdom's treasury.

Production and trade

Apart from its agricultural potential, Mesopotamia had few natural resources. But Mesopotamian artistic production was based on a far-flung web of interregional connections and its artisans turned out a variety of objects, large and small, in precious and base metals, semi-precious stones, hard woods, and other exotic materials that came from as far away as northeast Afghanistan and the Indus, the eastern Mediterranean and central Anatolia.

Money rings

In the Near East coined money was not used until the mid-first millennium BCE. But long before that, around 2100 BCE, silver coils of standard weight served as a unit of value and equivalency in Southern Mesopotamia. Change could be made by snipping off segments of a coil.

FACT
Mesopotamia is rich in petroleum, which seeps up to the surface in several places. The ancient Mesopotamians used this bitumen to caulk watercraft, seal jars, insert between brick courses in monumental buildings, and otherwise make objects waterproof.

Colonies

Around 3500 BCE, just as the Mesopotamian civilization was forming, small towns of completely Mesopotamian character, or in some cases Mesopotamian "enclaves" within local settlements, appeared in up-stream portions of the Euphrates and Tigris river drainages. Scholars connect these outposts of southern civilization with efforts to control the sources of raw materials that the new civilization was consuming in ever larger amounts.

Kingdoms of Mesopotamia

During its early history, Southern Mesopotamia was rarely politically unified. The region was divided among city-states or small kingdoms that shared a common culture, but they remained in constant struggle with each other. Three relatively brief periods of unity did occur between 3000 and 1600 BCE, for about 350 years in total, when Akkadian, Ur III, and old Babylonian rulers managed temporarily to subdue their neighbors and nearby parts of the region. Successful efforts in empire-building became more common, and the empires more durable, with the Late Bronze Age (1550–1200 BCE), when some of history's most famous empires appeared.

Late Bronze Age empires

The first of these empires – those of New Kingdom Egypt and of the Hittites based in central Anatolia – fought each other for control of the Canaanite kingdoms through the Levant (the eastern coast of the Mediterranean) and Syria. Hittite authority stretched from points on the Aegean Sea to northeastern Syria, and from the Anatolian Black Sea mountains to southern Syria. Egyptian power focused on the southern Levant and the Lebanese coast.

FACT
The Hittites used cuneiform writing for most purposes, but they also developed a system of hieroglyphs, unrelated to the Egyptian system, which they used for public inscriptions and royal seals. The subsequent "Neo-Hittite" kingdoms continued to use the hieroglyphic system until the seventh century BCE.

Canaanite civilization

The Canaanite civilization had developed around 2000 BCE. Like Mesopotamia, the Canaanite region encompassed different cultural and linguistic variations, but with a common core. Canaanite towns were often surrounded by massive earthen ramparts and stone walls. These fortified towns were the political and ritual centers of small kingdoms that included surrounding smaller settlements and agricultural land.

Canaanite religion

The Canaanite religion is vaguely familiar to a Bible-reading audience, because of the Old Testament's hostile references to it. The rich religious poetry from Ugarit, the capital of a small kingdom on the north Syrian coast, reveals an inside picture of El (the wise father of creation), Baal (god of rain, lord of thunderbolts and weapons), Athirat (El's consort, goddess of fertility), and other deities.

FACT
The Canaanite alphabet was so influential that scribes in Ugarit invented a cuneiform alphabet for writing their own language; they continued to use the more complicated traditional cuneiform for Akkadian texts.

Simplifying script

Canaanite scribes were conversant with the cuneiform script, and during the period of imperial domination they addressed letters in Akkadian to their Egyptian or Hittite overlords. But in the south a very different writing system developed – an alphabet of angular signs representing consonants, probably influenced by the Egyptians. The oldest examples of this alphabet appear in the deserts of Sinai and eastern Egypt, dated to about 1600 BCE. This radical intellectual innovation, which employed several dozen signs instead of the several hundred of cuneiform, established the basis for later alphabets including Greek and Latin, and ultimately our own.

The end of an era

The Hittite empire abruptly collapsed around 1200 BCE, and soon afterward the Egyptians withdrew from the southern Levant. A different world emerged from the ashes of these empires. Canaanite culture continued in some parts of the Levant, notably with the Phoenician cities along the Lebanese coast, but in Syria and southeast Anatolia new kingdoms formed under "Neo-Hittite" (cultural descendants of the Hittites) and Aramaean dynasties. To the south, in what is now the West Bank/Israel, the Israelites appeared.

Origins of Israel

Modern scholarship generally rejects the Biblical stories of exodus and invasion, but there is no agreement on an alternative account. One widely discussed view identifies the Israelites as internal Canaanite refugees, fleeing oppressive conditions, who established small villages in the central hills and developed a new cultural identity over time. A different view suggests that the Israelites were a herding people within the southern Levant, who settled in the uplands as the Canaanite city-states were breaking up. Whatever the correct interpretation may be, the archaeological record shows that during the several centuries following 1200 BCE, the central hills did hold numerous small villages. Larger walled towns with palace-like structures, formal gates, and other public buildings, reappeared around 950 BCE, and these works are commonly attributed to Solomon and the kingdom of Israel.

New empires

The Assyrian empire began taking shape around 900 BCE, when Assyrian armies began yearly campaigns of looting and tribute-extortion through the mountains to the east and north of Assyria, and across the lands to the west. At its peak, around 640 BCE, the Assyrian empire stretched from the Persian Gulf to central Anatolia, and from the Mediterranean Sea to western Iran. This empire crumbled when Babylonia sacked the Assyrian capital in 612 BCE, after having gained its independence. Babylon then took control of many provinces to create its own empire, which itself came to an end in 539 BCE when the Achaemenid Persians conquered Babylonia. The Persian empire was unprecedented in size: it stretched from Afghanistan, central Asia, and the Indus in the east to Thrace, the Levant, and Egypt in the west.

FACT

An archive of cuneiform tablets found at Tell el-Amarna, Akhenaten's capital on the Nile, includes diplomatic notes between Egypt and the contemporary Near Eastern powers, and hundreds of letters from vassal Canaanite kingdoms to their Egyptian overlord. These letters throw a vivid light on the political landscape of the Near East during the mid-fourteenth century BCE.

Artful boasts

The famous Assyrian wall reliefs – carved limestone panels that lined the walls of public rooms in palaces – showed the king carrying out his role of maintaining cosmic order: as a conqueror subduing peoples who refused to accept Assur, a ritual hunter of wild animals, and a performer of the cultic acts which assured the gods' benevolence and bounty. The Assyrian army vigorously pursued its "holy warfare," offering little mercy to resisters, especially rebel

LEFT Ancient Mesopotamian wall relief.

leaders; Assyria became almost synonymous with cruelty. The Persians were milder and their art less gory, with an emphasis on submission to the king as the personification of "truth" and order.

Imperial investments

Considerable wealth was invested in new imperial capitals. Assyrian kings built successive capitals at Kalhu (Nimrud), Khorsabad, and Nineveh; vast construction projects were completed in Babylon when it was the imperial center; and Persian kings created new capitals, at Parsagadae and Persepolis (both in Fars, Iran), and constructed sumptuous palaces at Susa and Babylon. These building projects used costly materials and employed the skills of craftsmen from across the empire.

Palaces: *Palace contents were opulent, with Assyria providing the best examples. In addition to the lavish wall reliefs, enormous human-headed, winged bulls and lions guarded the main doorways against evil spirits.*

Furniture: *Wooden furniture was ornamented with ivory inlays carved in the styles of the western provinces and of Assyria itself.*

Burials: *Graves of royal women beneath the floors of a palace in Nimrud contained masses of gold jewelry and semi-precious stones.*

Literature: *A palace at Nineveh contained a vast library of cuneiform tablets, the accumulated literature and wisdom of the Mesopotamian civilization.*

Assyrian siege ramp
Assyrian warfare involved a variety of tactics for besieging the strongholds of their enemies. One tactic was the construction (under fire) of an earthen ramp up to the top of a town wall. The remains of a siege ramp are still visible today at Lachish in modern Israel. It is thought to have been constructed in 701 BCE; the same siege ramp is depicted on a palace wall relief in Nineveh.

Phoenician traders
The Phoenicians were a part of all three of the early empires. They were famous both for their craft products at home (carved ivories, glass, purple dye, metalwork), and for their colonies and commercial activities across the Mediterranean Sea. The Phoenicians had earlier established a few colonies in the eastern Mediterranean, but after they became part of the Assyrian empire they created many more colonies further west. This "mercantile empire" facilitated a flow of both raw materials (notably iron) and finished goods from the western Mediterranean to Phoenicia, which in turn helped the Phoenician cities to meet tribute obligations to their imperial overlords.

FACT

The ninth-century Assyrian king Assurnasirpal II constructed a magnificent new capital at Kalhu (Nimrud), and inaugurated it with a banquet which – he claimed – nearly 70,000 people attended.

Arabian traders

The South Arabian civilization took form between 1000 and 800 BCE along the desert margins of modern Yemen. The early South Arabian kingdoms, notably Saba (Sheba), grew rich from carrying frankincense, myrrh, and other costly products to consumers in the Levant and Mesopotamia. This trade connection introduced northern ideas to South Arabia, including a version of the Canaanite alphabet and Mesopotamian religious symbols and sculptural styles.

Arabian queens

Arab societies lived along the southern fringes of the Neo-Assyrian empire, and often paid tribute to it. The Assyrian records refer to women who led several Arab groups. These women were perhaps parallels to the "Queen of Sheba" who visited Solomon.

RIGHT A depiction of the Queen of Sheba arriving in Israel.

FACT
In many parts of the Near East, unbaked mud brick was the most common building material. When mud brick buildings collapse they create thick deposits of earth that surround the stubs of walls. Over time a stratified mound accumulates; these artificial hills are called *tells* in Arabic, *tels* in Hebrew, *tepes* in Persian and *höyüks* in Turkish.

End of an era

The Persian empire marked the beginning of a new historical phase of both regional and world history, in which imperial ambitions were played out on a much larger scale. After Alexander the Macedonian had exhausted his ambitions of world domination, his generals split the former Achaemenid territories into several, often conflicting, parts. Eventually Rome occupied the western territories, and confronted in their turn the Parthian and Sassanian inheritors of the eastern territories, whose power centers lay more in Iran and central Asia than in Mesopotamia. Almost incidental to these political and military contests, the ancient Mesopotamian civilization of ziggurats, cuneiform, and cylinder seals withered and died.

Medes and Persians

The Medes and Persians were cattle-herding peoples who spoke Indo-European languages. They moved from Central Asia into western Iran late in the second millennium BCE. The Medes settled in the Zagros mountains, whereas the Persians moved further south to Fars (southern Iran), and eventually created the Achaemenid empire.

EGYPT

Early settlements

Egypt is a long, thin country in the northeast corner of Africa. The Nile – a wide, deep river – flows northward along a valley running through the center of Egypt. The river divides in the north to form the flat, triangular Nile Delta. To either side of the Nile Valley there is fertile land, bounded by deserts, and finally steep mountains. The greater part of ancient Egypt's population lived near the banks of the Nile where the arable agricultural land was, and still is, found.

Many thousands of years ago people started to settle alongside the River Nile. The Nile became a highway for boats and a drain for sewage. The mud along the riverbank was an extremely useful building material. Nile water was used for cooking, washing, and laundry, and the fish in the Nile were a free source of healthy food. Freed from the struggle to irrigate their land, and with plentiful natural resources, the Egyptians quickly evolved a dynastic society which lasted, more or less unbroken, for over 3,000 years.

Unification

Agriculture began in Egypt in around 5450 BCE, converting the Stone Age people from hunter-gatherers to farmers. With agriculture came permanent settlement and the first recognizably Egyptian

Timeline

c. 2920–2649 BCE
Early Dynastic Period: Dynasties 1–2
Emergence of the unified Egypt
Development of hieroglyphic writing

c. 2134–2040 BCE
First Intermediate Period: Dynasties 9–11
Collapse of national unity
Warlords rule mini kingdoms in Egypt

c. 2649–2134 BCE
Old Kingdom: Dynasties 3–8
The Sakkara Step pyramid
The Giza pyramids and Sphinx

c. 2040–1640 BCE
Middle Kingdom: Dynasties 11–14
Arts and literature flourish
Pyramids continue as royal tombs

communities. The Badarians (4500–4000 BCE) brought farming to the Nile Valley. Initially contemporary with the Badarian culture, the Naqada phase lasted between 4000 and 3050 BCE. By late Naqada times Egypt could boast one homogeneous material culture with little regional variation. The Naqada people lived in wealthy independent city-states and their satellite farming communities.

Early kings

The names of three early kings have been recovered from Naqada contexts. Iri-Hor and Ka both have tombs in the royal Abydos cemetery but Egyptologists cannot be certain that they ruled a united land. Narmer, however, is depicted wearing the white and red crowns which signify Upper (or southern) and Lower (or northern) Egypt. Narmer is therefore classified as Egypt's first king.

Menes

Legend tells how the southern warrior Menes raised an army and marched northward, conquering city after city until Egypt was united. However there is little evidence of a civil war at the end of the Naqada period. Instead, it seems that Egypt enjoyed a sustained period of political and commercial consolidation followed, perhaps, by a series of short battles.

1640–1550 BCE
cond Intermediate Period:
nasties 15–17, Hyksos kings
quer northern Egypt

c. 1070–712 BCE
Third Intermediate Period:
Dynasties 21–25, Priests of
Amen rule southern Egypt

332–30 BCE
Macedonian and Ptolemaic
Period, Reigns of Alexander
the Great and Cleopatra VII

c. 1550–1070 BCE
New Kingdom: Dynasties 18–20
Royal tombs in the Valley of the Kings
The Amarna period

c. 712–332 BCE
Late Period: Dynasties 25–31
Nubian kings conquer Egypt

Dynastic Egypt Chart*

EARLY DYNASTIC PERIOD: DYNASTIES 1–2	(c. 2920–2649)
1st Dynasty	(c. 2920–2770)
2nd Dynasty	(c. 2770–2649)
OLD KINGDOM: DYNASTIES 3–8	(c. 2649–2134)
3rd Dynasty	(c. 2649–2575)
4th Dynasty	(c. 2575–2465)
5th Dynasty	(c. 2465–2323)
6th Dynasty	(c. 2323–2150)
7th and 8th Dynasties	(c. 2150–2134)
FIRST INTERMEDIATE PERIOD: DYNASTIES 9–11	(c. 2134–2040)
MIDDLE KINGDOM: DYNASTIES 11–14	(c. 2040–1640)
11th Dynasty – national rule	(c. 2040–1991)
12th Dynasty	(c. 1991–1783)
13th and 14th Dynasties	(c. 1783–1640)
SECOND INTERMEDIATE PERIOD: DYNASTIES 15–17	(c. 1640–1550)
NEW KINGDOM: DYNASTIES 18–20	(c. 1550–1070)
18th Dynasty	(c. 1550–1307)
19th Dynasty	(c. 1307–1196)
20th Dynasty	(c. 1196–1070)
THIRD INTERMEDIATE PERIOD: DYNASTIES 21–25	(c. 1070–712)
LATE PERIOD: DYNASTIES 25–31	(c. 712–332)
25th (Nubian) Dynasty – national rule	(c. 712–664)
26th (Saite) Dynasty	(664–525)
27th (1st Persian) Dynasty	(525–404)
28th Dynasty	(404–399)
29th Dynasty	(399–380)
30th Dynasty	(380–343)
31st (2nd Persian) Dynasty	(343–332)
MACEDONIAN AND PTOLEMAIC PERIOD	(332–30)

*All years are BCE

The Old Kingdom
(c. 2649–2134 BCE: Third to Eighth Dynasties)

Djoser was the first king of the Third Dynasty, when Egypt became a prosperous country through agriculture and trade. He chose to be buried in an impressive funerary complex, which included a step pyramid, a warren of underground galleries, and a series of open courts lined with shrines. He built in stone instead of the traditional mud-brick. Pyramid building would be the defining characteristic of the next 500 years, and the constant demand for materials would stimulate the economy and encourage craftsmen to aspire to new technical and artistic heights.

Pyramids

The kings of the Old and Middle Kingdoms built pyramid tombs in the desert cemeteries to the west of their capitals. The pyramids were the most visible part of their funerary complexes, which also included a valley temple opening onto a canal, a lengthy causeway, and a mortuary temple next to the pyramids. Pyramid building was connected with the cult of the sun god Re of Heliopolis. This interest in solar religion became most obvious during the Fifth Dynasty, when several kings built sun temples. Queen consorts were buried in small pyramids erected as a part of their husband's complex. The purpose of the pyramids is nowhere explained. But Egyptologists believe that they may have served as gigantic ramps that would allow the soul of the dead king to travel up into the sky.

Disintegration

Toward the end of the Old Kingdom the bureaucracy had grown enormous and unwieldy. The land, once so fertile, was experiencing increasing aridity, and a period of low Nile flood levels was having a drastic effect on the crops. As confidence in the royal family declined local governors grew increasingly powerful. The ephemeral Seventh and Eighth Dynasties saw Egypt ruled by a series of powerless kings before central authority collapsed and Egypt fragmented.

The Middle Kingdom
(c. 2040–1640 BCE: 11th to 14th Dynasties)

The scribe Ipuwer tells us that the First Intermediate Period (Ninth to Eleventh Dynasties) was a time of chaos, when crime was rife and the Nile ran red with blood. But Ipuwer exaggerated. Although there were occasional food shortages, evidence from the provincial cemeteries confirms that life for many people improved at this time.

Rise and fall

Slowly, the independent local governors started to form alliances until two dominant dynasties emerged; a northern dynasty at Herakleopolis and a southern dynasty at Thebes. The Theban Mentuhotep II reunited Egypt and established a new northern capital city, Itj-Tawy. The Middle Kingdom became a time of renewed prosperity. Literature and the arts flourished and there were military and trading missions beyond Egypt's borders. But these were difficult times for the wider Mediterranean world, and Egypt started to attract migrants who formed independent communities in the Egyptian Delta. A succession of weak kings heralded the collapse of central authority, and the Middle Kingdom failed.

Southern Egypt was now sandwiched between the Nubian Kingdom of Kush and the Canaanite Hyksos kings who ruled from the Delta. The Theban king Ahmose marched north to expel the Hyksos, chasing them across the Sinai Peninsula into Canaan.

The creation of the world

In the beginning only the waters of chaos existed. Deep within the waters floated a perfect egg. Suddenly the egg cracked open and a mound rose out of the waters. Seated on that mound was Atum. Atum had created himself. Now he set about creating the living. From the fluids of his body emerged twin children, Shu, the god of the dry air and his sister-wife Tefnut, goddess of moisture. Atum, Shu and Tefnut lived safe on their island-mound in the midst of the dark sea of chaos.

FACT

Tall papyrus plants grew in the marshy Nile Delta. The triangular papyrus stalks, sliced into strips and pressed together, made a valuable form of "paper" for Egypt's scribes.

Hieroglyphs

The ancient Egyptians did not use an alphabet. Instead they used pictures or signs to represent sounds and make words. An example of this, *The Book of the Dead* from the Ramesside Period, was written in a form of the hieroglyphic script. Hieroglyphs were mainly used for official documents during the Old and Middle Egyptian periods. The most important of the hieroglyph signs are the twenty-four monosyllabic consonant signs, some of which have variants, illustrated over the page. Confusingly, the script can be read horizontally from left to right, horizontally from right to left, vertically facing left to right, or vertically facing right to left. Many of the signs have a definite front or back, for instance a person, which makes determining the direction quite easy in practise.

LEFT
Egyptian hieroglyphs.

Egyptian Hieroglyphs

A sample of the monsyllabic consonant signs, the most important of the ancient Egyptian signs.

Sign	Description	Transliteration	Spoken value
	Vulture	*ꜣ*	A
	Reed	*i*	I
	Double reed	*y*	Y
	Arm	*ꜥ*	A
	Quail chick	*w*	W
	Coil of rope	*w*	W
	Leg	*b*	B
	Stool	*p*	P
	Horned viper	*f*	F
	Owl	*m*	M
	Water	*n*	n
	Mouth	*r*	r
	Reed hut	*h*	h
	Twisted flax	*ḥ*	h
	Placenta	*ḫ*	kh
	Animal's belly	*ẖ*	kh
	Door bolt	*s*	s
	Fold of cloth	*s*	s
	Lake	*š*	sh

The New Kingdom
(c. 1550–1070 BCE: 18th to 20th Dynasties)

The early 18th Dynasty monarchs annexed Nubia and much of the Near East, creating an empire stretching from Nubia to Syria. The New Kingdom pharaohs lived in Thebes, far from the traditional northern royal cemeteries. Abandoning the pyramid form, they built hidden rock-cut tombs in the remote Valley of the Kings. Initially, it was hoped that these tombs would provide greater security for the dead kings and their valuable grave goods, but the only royal tomb to survive substantially intact was that of Tutankhamen, which was accidentally covered in rubble when Ramesses VI built his tomb. The workmen's village of Deir el-Medina was established to house the royal tomb workers. They also built impressive temples on the edge of the cultivated land of the Valley of the Kings.

Hatshepsut

Hatshepsut was the daughter of the 18th Dynasty ruler Tuthmosis I and the sister-wife of Tuthmosis II. She was Egypt's most successful queen, ruling alongside her stepson-nephew Tuthmosis III for nearly 20 years (c.1473–1458 BCE.) Her reign was a time of peace and prosperity, with an extensive building program and a successful trading mission to the land of Punt. Hatshepsut's Theban mortuary temple at Deir el-Bahari is one of Egypt's most unusual and beautiful buildings. However, despite such achievements, after her death her name and images were erased, and her reign was quickly forgotten.

Akhenaten and Nefertiti

Akhenaten (reigned c.1353–1335 BCE) was the 18th Dynasty "heretic king" formerly known as Amenhotep IV. Akhenaten abandoned Egypt's traditional pantheon and devoted himself to the worship of a hitherto unremarkable sun god known as The Aten. The Aten took the form of a faceless sun disk high in the sky. Akhenaten built a new capital city, Akhetaten (modern Amarna) in Middle Egypt. He and his consort Nefertiti had six daughters but no

LEFT The funery mask of Tutankhamen, found by Howard Carter's team in 1922.

sons. Some Egyptologists believe that Nefertiti ruled alongside her husband, and that she perhaps reigned alone after his death. Although his successors restored the old gods, and the old capital, the dynastic line was failing, and so ended the 18th Dynasty.

Tutankhamen

Howard Carter's 1922 discovery of his virtually intact tomb has made Tutankhamen Egypt's best-known king. However we know surprisingly little about the "boy king." We do not know who his parents were, although it seems likely that they were the 18th Dynasty king Akhenaten and his secondary queen Kiya. We do know that Tutankhamen was married to Ankhesenamen, the daughter of Akhenaten and Nefertiti. After perhaps 10 years on the throne (c. 1333–1323 BCE) Tutankhamen died unexpectedly, and was buried in a small non-royal tomb in the Valley of the Kings.

Ramesses I and II

The 19th Dynasty dawned with the accession of Ramesses I. Ramesses II "the Great," his grandson, also ruled Egypt during the 19th Dynasty (c. 1290–1224 BCE.) His reign saw a series of impressive military campaigns and an extensive building program in both Egypt and Nubia. Ramesses had many wives – the best known being Nefertari and Iset-Nofret – and an estimated 100 children! Proud of his fertility, he decorated his temples with images of the young princes and princesses. Ramesses ruled Egypt for over 65 years and lived to be over 90 years of age. Many of his children died before him, and he was eventually succeeded by his thirteenth-born son, Merenptah.

End of the New Kingdom

But Ramesses' death left Egypt unsettled. This was a time of growing international insecurity. Pirates menaced the Mediterranean coast, the Delta was threatened by bands of nomadic Libyans, and the empire was crumbling. Ramesses III modeled his reign on that of Ramesses II. But as the empire shrank, the loss of taxes and the closure of international trade routes made a significant hole in the economy. Meanwhile poor harvests led to inflation, corruption, and civil unrest. A further eight Ramesses succeeded to the throne, but the New Kingdom ended with the death of Ramesses XI.

The Late Period
(c. 712–332 BCE: 25th–31st Dynasties)

Large numbers of Libyans settled in Egypt during the Third Intermediate Period (c. 1070–712 BCE). Despite the inevitable tensions, this was for many a time of peace and prosperity characterized by the perfection of the art of mummification. Smendes, first king of the 21st Dynasty, claimed sovereignty over the whole land but the High Priest of Amen Herihor and his descendants effectively controlled southern Egypt from Thebes.

Declining stability

The 22nd Dynasty saw the throne pass to Shoshenq I, a king of Libyan extraction. A reduction in the status of the High Priest brought stability. But Egypt soon started to fragment, and the Nubian king Piye marched north to be crowned king. His dynasty came to an abrupt halt when the Assyrians invaded. The puppet king Necho I ruled briefly alongside his son Psamtik. As the Nubians attempted to reclaim Egypt, Necho was killed and Psamtik escaped to Nineveh, before returning to take his father's place. The resulting 26th Dynasty achieved a century of peace until, in 525 BCE, Cambyses II of Persia invaded Egypt.

After over a century of Persian rule, there was a short period of native Egyptian rule (28th–30th Dynasties) before the 30th Dynasty ended with a second Persian invasion. In 332 BCE, Alexander the Great claimed Egypt.

Alexander The Great – King of Egypt

Alexander III "the Great" conquered Egypt in 332, ending almost two centuries of intermittent Persian rule. Legend tells that he chose to be crowned by Egyptian priests in the temple of the creator god Ptah of Memphis. Soon after, visiting the oracle of Zeus-Ammon in the Siwa Oasis, he received divine confirmation of his right to rule. In 331 BCE Alexander founded the seaport of Alexandria. Alexander died in Babylon on June 10, 323 BCE; his body was subsequently kidnapped by Ptolemy I and displayed in a mausoleum in Alexandria.

FACT

New Kingdom tomb scenes show semi-naked female dancers performing gymnastic routines to entertain the elite as they dine. These may be interpreted as scenes of sexual potency and rebirth.

The Ptolemies (304–30 BCE)

After the unexpected death of Alexander the Great in 323 BCE, the Egyptian throne passed first to his brother, Philip Arrhidaeus, and then to his posthumous son, Alexander IV. The murder of the younger Alexander saw the end of his line. As Alexander's empire fragmented, the Macedonian general Ptolemy seized control of Egypt, ruling as Ptolemy I Soter "The Savior." A further 14 Ptolemies would follow. By the time Cleopatra VII was born in 69 BCE, her family had ruled Egypt from the Mediterranean seaport of Alexandria for two and a half centuries.

Cleopatra VII

Cleopatra was the daughter of Ptolemy XII Auletes. She came to the throne in 51 BCE ruling alongside her brother, Ptolemy XIII, but was deposed and forced to flee to Syria. Julius Caesar restored Cleopatra to her throne alongside her younger brother Ptolemy XIV. Cleopatra bore Caesar a son, Ptolemy Caesar. Following Caesar's assassination, Cleopatra formed a liaison with Mark Antony and bore him three children. Their plans for an eastern empire collapsed following their defeat at the naval battle of Actium, and both Antony and Cleopatra committed suicide in 30 BCE.

End of the Dynasties

The majority of the Egyptian people still lived in mud-brick villages, producing the grain and flax that underpinned the economy. But times were changing. Rome, not Egypt, dominated the Mediterranean world, and the old aristocracy in Egypt's cities had been thrust into the background as Greeks started to run the country. This new cosmopolitanism was reflected in the architecture, as buildings developed a distinct Hellenistic style. Greek was spoken with increasing frequency and coinage was introduced, unknown during the earlier dynastic age when all transactions were conducted by barter. The death of Cleopatra VII in 32 BCE saw the end of the dynastic age.

The Rosetta Stone

The Rosetta Stone was discovered in 1799 at Fort Julien (Borg Rashid) in the Nile Delta. The stone was a large, damaged, granite slab inscribed with three copies of a decree commemorating the accession of Ptolemy V. One copy was a readable Greek text written in Greek characters. Above this came two versions written in the ancient Egyptian language using different writing styles: the cursive demotic script, and hieroglyphs. In 1822 the French linguist Jean-François Champollion was able to use the Rosetta Stone to decode the hitherto unreadable hieroglyphic and demotic scripts.

LEFT The Rosetta Stone, carved in c. 196 BCE, was found by French soldiers. It is currently housed in the British Museum in London, UK.

ABOVE Detail.

FACT
Elite Egyptian villas had bathrooms equipped with shower cubicles, toilets, and drains. As all houses were built from mud-brick, the bathrooms were lined with stone.

Gods and goddesses

Egypt was a polytheistic land with over 1,000 gods. Some of these gods appeared fully human, or fully animal in form. Others were shown with a human body topped by an animal head. This convention allowed artists to depict animal gods sitting on thrones, receiving offerings, shaking sacred rattles, and otherwise behaving like their human-bodied counterparts.

FACT

The Great Sphinx of Giza, a crouching lion with a king's head, was carved by the Fourth Dynasty pharaoh Khaefre. Other sphinxes had ram or hawk heads.

State gods

Some gods, such as Re, Osiris, Isis, and Hathor, may be classified as state gods. These were deities who were worshipped in major state-funded temples throughout Egypt. Technically, these gods could only be worshipped by the king – the one mortal who could communicate with the divine. In theory, the king of Egypt was responsible for making all the offerings in all the temples. In practise this was impossible, and kings were allowed to appoint priests who could make offerings on their behalf. The ordinary Egyptians had little or no access to the state gods, and were not welcomed into their temples.

Demi-gods

Other gods may be classified as demi-gods, or local gods. They played a significant role in the lives of the ordinary Egyptian. A pregnant woman, for example, might call upon the magical dwarf Bes or the combined hippopotamus-crocodile goddess Taweret for help in labor, while a villager with a problem might consult a local oracle.

Egyptian gods

Re *A hawk, or a hawk-headed man. Re is a creator god and a sun god. Every day he sails across the sky in his solar boat.*

Hathor *A beautiful woman, a cow, or a cow-headed woman. Hathor represents love, music, motherhood, and drunkenness.*

ABOVE Re was a major deity in Egypt.

Osiris *A mummified human body with an unwrapped head, a crown, and beard. The living Osiris ruled Egypt. After death, he became king of the Afterlife.*

Isis *A beautiful woman, who sometimes takes the form of a bird. Isis is a powerful magician and healer. She is the wife of Osiris and protects his son Horus.*

Thoth *An ibis or a baboon (or occasionally a human body with an ibis or baboon head.) Thoth is the scribe of the gods.*

Amen *A man wearing a kilt and crown; occasionally he appears as a ram or a goose. Amen is the warrior god of the New Kingdom.*

ABOVE Wall painting of the Isis, dating from c.1360 BCE.

The Karnak Temple

The extensive Karnak Temple complex at Thebes is the largest of Egypt's surviving temples. The complex was home to the god Amen, "the hidden one," his goddess wife Mut, and their divine son Khonsu. Included within the complex were shrines dedicated to the gods Ptah, Maat, and Montu, and a large sacred lake. The complex was in use during the Middle Kingdom, but was massively extended during the New Kingdom, when successive pharaohs vied with each other to make the most impressive improvements to the site.

Mummification

The Egyptians believed that the soul could live beyond death if the body also survived. Natural mummification could be achieved by burying the dead in simple pit graves dug directly into the hot desert sands. But the elite Egyptians wanted coffins, and tombs to hold their grave goods, and these separated the bodies from the hot sands,

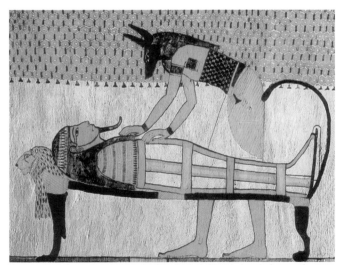

ABOVE A wall painting showing Anubis, the jackal-headed god of mummification.

FACT

Linen thread was spun from flax. Egypt had an almost insatiable demand for linen, which was used to make garments, rope, and the bandages used in mummification.

causing them to rot. The undertakers therefore developed a method of artificially preserving the body by removing the soft organs, drying the body in natron salt, then applying many layers of linen bandages.

Crime and punishment

Decorated private tombs show scenes of happy families working in the fields, feasting, and playing games. It is an idyllic existence. But it is not an accurate reflection of daily life. Ancient Egypt had more than her fair share of thefts, assaults, and murders, and there is evidence for a trend of ever-increasing crime levels and progressively more brutal punishments as the dynasties progress. To deal with crime, the courts had the power to interrogate with force. Those found guilty might suffer banishment, mutilation, or death by impaling with a wooden spike.

The farming life

The Nile allowed Egypt's farmers to grow crops in an otherwise arid region. Every year, from July to October, the river burst her banks, covering the fields with muddy water. The towns and cities, prudently built on high ground, became little islands linked by raised paths. The waters retreated in late October, leaving the fields ready for planting. The farmers sowed their crops and waited. In late spring they gathered a wonderful harvest. The land was then sterilized by the hot sun, before the river flooded again in July.

SOUTH
ASIA

Indus civilization

In the early third millennium BCE there were three differing traditions in the Greater Indus region, in the south, north, and east. Between 2600 and 2500 BCE these became united, creating the Indus (or Harappan) civilization, perhaps through the adoption of a shared ideology, and there was a cultural transformation which included considerable standardization and the emergence of writing. Most existing settlements were abandoned, or destroyed and rebuilt, and new settlements founded following uniform principles: the streets were orientated in the cardinal directions, a part of the settlement (the "citadel") was separately walled and often elevated, and fine water supply and drainage systems were installed. Towns and cities were often built on brick platforms and walled to protect them against the unpredictable floods of the major rivers.

The Indus civilization was most probably a single state, though some scholars suggest it may have been a confederacy of several smaller states. It covered a far larger area than its contemporaries in Mesopotamia and Egypt, stretching from Gujarat and the Makran coast to the Himalayan foothills and the Delhi region. Perhaps uniquely, no warfare seems to have been involved in the creation, continued existence, or fall of this civilization.

Timeline

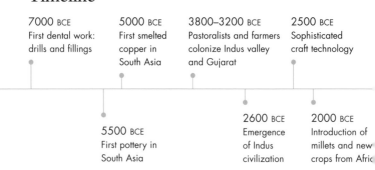

7000 BCE
First dental work: drills and fillings

5000 BCE
First smelted copper in South Asia

3800–3200 BCE
Pastoralists and farmers colonize Indus valley and Gujarat

2500 BCE
Sophisticated craft technology

5500 BCE
First pottery in South Asia

2600 BCE
Emergence of Indus civilization

2000 BCE
Introduction of millets and new crops from Afric

Settlements

Five cities developed in key locations: Harappa, Mohenjo-daro, and Dholavira along the main artery, the Indus, and Ganweriwala and Rakhigarhi on the parallel Saraswati river system (now largely dry.) All exceeded 200 acres (80 hectares); in contrast, towns were generally under 40 acres (16 hectares.) Towns and specialized industrial villages were also strategically located, facilitating a highly efficient internal distribution network that spread the products of different regions throughout the Indus realms. These included fine flint from the Rohri hills (Sindh), shell bangles and dried fish from the coast, beads and ivory from Gujarat, and copper from the adjacent Arawalli hills. Many farming villages grew wheat, barley, pulses, cotton, and other crops, and raised cattle, along with a few sheep, goats, buffaloes, and chickens. Pastoralists moving their herds between seasonal grazing grounds acted as trade carriers, and goods were also transported by boat.

FACT

Unlike most ancient houses, those in Indus towns and cities often had toilets as well as fine bathrooms.

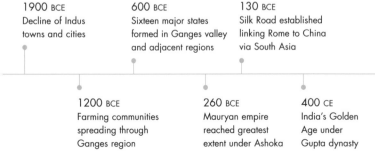

1900 BCE
Decline of Indus
towns and cities

600 BCE
Sixteen major states
formed in Ganges valley
and adjacent regions

130 BCE
Silk Road established
linking Rome to China
via South Asia

1200 BCE
Farming communities
spreading through
Ganges region

260 BCE
Mauryan empire
reached greatest
extent under Ashoka

400 CE
India's Golden
Age under
Gupta dynasty

Harappa and Mohenjo-daro

Harappa, in the Punjab, comprised a number of separate sectors with impressive walls and gateways and a large range of industries. Some of its citizens were buried in an extramural cemetery. The largest city was Mohenjo-daro, originally around 620 acres (250 hectares): only a fraction of this is visible today above the deep Indus alluvium. Public architecture on its citadel included a large pillared hall, perhaps for public meetings, a building thought to be a warehouse, and the Great Bath, a skillfully constructed watertight basin in which religious ceremonies probably took place. Water was also important in the residential area, where there were some 700 wells. The two- or three-storeyed houses were built around courtyards, and had bathrooms and efficient drains. No temples or palaces have been found, here or elsewhere, and the Harappan political organization remains a mystery.

The coast

Water was universally important. Within the massive stone walls of Dholavira, built on an island in Gujarat, there were at least 16 vast reservoirs with earth and stone embankments. The citadel was divided in two, each part with impressive walls and gateways; in one were found the remains of a wooden signboard bearing an inscription in large white script.

FACT
The enigmatic Indus script still defies translation, guarding its secrets. It is likely that most Indus writing was on perishable materials, now long vanished.

Trade

In the small town of Lothal, further south, many of the houses contained workshops, which produced a large range of goods for local or wider Indus use, or for exchange with hunter-gatherers who supplied materials such as honey, ivory, and perhaps Indian silk. The town's warehouse was destroyed by fire, preserving sealings from the many packages stored here.

Lothal is usually called a port, on dubious evidence: a brick-lined basin here has been variously interpreted as a dock or a reservoir but its true purpose remains baffling. Harappan ports are known elsewhere in Gujarat and further north in the Makran. The Harappans sailed from these ports to Oman to trade for copper. They also sailed through the Persian Gulf as far as Sumer, to which they exported many manufactured goods and valuable materials including timber, gold, and lapis lazuli, perhaps in return for fine woollen textiles and silver.

Crafts

Jewelry played an important part in Indus dress, as the many lively terracotta figurines show.

Shell bangles *were manufactured in huge quantities in industrial villages and urban workshops. Bangles were also made of terracotta, copper, and faience (glazed pottery), reflecting highly developed pyrotechnical skills.*

Beads *Skill was also displayed in the manufacture of vast numbers of beads, mainly of gemstones. As well as the famed "etched" (actually bleached) carnelian*

ABOVE Typically, this mother goddess figurine from Mohenjo-daro wears an elaborate headdress and many necklaces.

beads, fine products included exceptionally long carnelian beads, each requiring a fortnight's work, and minute steatite beads which were less than 1/16 inches (1–3 millimeters) in diameter.

Stamp seals *Steatite was also made into beautiful square stamp seals bearing an inscription, probably the name or title of the owner, and a design, usually of an animal. The unicorn was most common; others included zebu bulls, rhinoceroses, and elephants.*

Disintegration

From around 2000 BCE, changes brought about the break-up of the Indus state and the decline or abandonment of urban life and associated features, notably writing. Probable causes include disease, reduced flow in the Saraswati irrigation system, and a major shift to the cultivation of summer crops, especially rice and African millets. Much of the central area saw depopulation, but settlement density increased in Gujarat and the eastern region.

FACT
An Akkadian seal found in Mesopotamia belonged to an interpreter of the Indus language.

Mauryan empire

Farmers spread eventually into the Ganges basin, where by the sixth century BCE small states were emerging – the Mahajanapadas. This was a period of great social and religious reform, inspired by the Buddha and the Jain saint Mahavira. Conflict and competition gradually increased the extent of some states and reduced their number, strategically-placed Magadha becoming the most successful. In 321 BCE its ruler, Chandragupta Maurya, founded the Mauryan empire which came to control most of South Asia.

Spread of Buddhism

Maurya's grandson, Ashoka, experienced deep remorse for the destruction wrought by war and became a Buddhist convert. During his long reign he promoted the well-being of his subjects, patronized religious groups, and constructed pillars, known today as Ashokan pillars, commemorating important places in the Buddha's life, and reputedly 84,000 stupas (relic mounds) covering corporeal relics of the Buddha, as well as erecting inscriptions recording his noble intentions. Evangelical missions, some led by members of Ashoka's family, spread Buddhism to other lands.

FACT

As well as providing for his human subjects, Ashoka founded hospitals to treat injured and sick animals.

Angkor

Angkor was the capital of south-east Asia's Khmer Empire from the ninth century BCE to the fifteenth century CE, when it was pillaged by neighboring Siam. It was not a city, but a huge, sprawling complex of temples, monuments, reservoirs, and canals, that developed in different stages over the centuries. It seems likely that a fall in agricultural production may have been a factor in the downfall of Angkorian civilization, along with the military expansion of the Siamese.

Angkor Monuments

Angkor Thom *The Khmer kingdom reached its greatest extent under Jayavarman VII who built the huge complex of Angkor Thom in the twelfth century CE. This complex covers 3.5 square miles (9 km²), and is enclosed by a wall nearly two miles (three kilometers) on each side. Each side is pierced by a great gateway, 75 feet (23 meters) high, which features* a tower carved with four faces pointing to the four directions; each gate is approached by an impressive avenue of carved gods and demons carrying a giant serpent across the moat.

Bayon One of the greatest monuments of Angkor, the Bayon, is characterized by 54 towers, each with four smiling faces of a future Buddha, and extensive bas-reliefs of scenes from Khmer life, as well as events in Khmer history, including great naval battles.

Angkor Wat The most famous temple complex of all, Angkor Wat, was built in the twelfth century CE. This great temple blended Hindu cosmology and architecture with pre-existing Khmer beliefs. The enclosure symbolizes the Hindu cosmos, while the temple itself stood for the five peaks of Mount Meru, the abode of the gods.

ABOVE The Angkor Wat temple complex.

FAR
EAST

Beginning of Chinese civilization

The legends that record the founding of China tell of three mythical creators. Sheng Nong, the "Divine farmer," is purported to have invented agriculture implements, such as the plow and hoe. Fu Xi, known as the "Ox-tamer," domesticated the animals and created the family. Huang Di, the "Yellow ruler," created the bow and arrow, boats, ceramics, silk, and writing. He was also the first of the five great pre-dynastic rulers, the last ones being Yao and Shun.

Prehistory

Around 10,000 years ago people moved from a nomadic economy of gathering and hunting to one of food production, with the cultivation of grain. By 5000 BCE, six Neolithic cultures with agriculture, pottery, and villages had emerged in many of the river valleys, such as the Yellow river in the north, with mostly millet cultivation, and the Yangzi river in the south, with mostly rice agriculture. Archaeological discoveries from these cultures have revealed refined painted ceramic products, such as from the Yangshao culture (c. 5000–3000 BCE) and spectacular jades from the Hongshan and Liangzhu cultures (between 3500 and 2500 BCE.)

Timeline

100,000 BCE
Homo erectus
(Peking man)
in China

3000–2000 BCE
Late Neolithic
Cultures, heyday
of jade

551–c. 479 BCE
Confucius, China's
first moral
philosopher

403 BCE
Warring States
Period

10,000 BCE
Early Neolithic Cultures
(such as Yangshao,
Hongshan, Liangzhu)

1600 BCE
Shang Dynasty, heyday
of the Bronze Age culture

221 BCE
The State of
Qin unifies
China

FACT
In the Hongshan and Liangzhu cultures, jade was fashioned into objects with ritual and religious meaning, such as small figurines of turtles, birds, so-called pig-dragons, *bi*-disks, or *cong*-columns. The *bi* and *cong* jades were considered to have cosmological significance.

Earliest Noodles

Archaeologists have uncovered the world's oldest known noodles, dating back 4000 years, at an archaeological site, Lajia, along the upper reaches of the Yellow river in north-west China. Previously, the earliest evidence of this food staple had been a Chinese written description of noodle preparation dating back a mere 1900 years.

The 20-inch (50-cm) yellow strands were found in an upturned pot that had probably been buried during a catastrophic flood. The shapes of the noodles could still be clearly recognized.

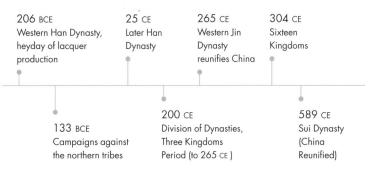

206 BCE
Western Han Dynasty, heyday of lacquer production

25 CE
Later Han Dynasty

265 CE
Western Jin Dynasty reunifies China

304 CE
Sixteen Kingdoms

133 BCE
Campaigns against the northern tribes

200 CE
Division of Dynasties, Three Kingdoms Period (to 265 CE)

589 CE
Sui Dynasty (China Reunified)

The Shang Dynasty (1600–1050 BCE)

Along with permanent settlements, new forms of social organization arose in China, and around 2000 BCE in the area of the Middle Yellow River a more complex Bronze-Age civilization emerged. The earliest bronze vessels, such as goblets, vases, or steamers, were found at Erlitou, a region attributed to the earliest stage of dynastic China, the still highly-debated Xia dynasty.

The first well-documented and archaeologically traceable dynasty is the Shang. For the first time large-scale cities, such as Anyang and Zhengzhou, were political and religious centers of the state-like structure. Domestication of the horse, bronze casting, and cultivation of grain were the main achievements of the Shang period.

Writing

Exactly when writing was first used in China is not known. Symbols or emblems on Neolithic ceramics may be seen as early Chinese characters. The earliest evidence of characters in full sentences is found on oracle bones. From the look of the characters it is clear that the Shang used a writing system still in use today. Among the characters, which number more than 1,000, some are pictographs representing a thing or idea, while others are used for their sound.

Tomb of Lady Hao at Anyang

The only royal Shang tomb never to be robbed was tomb number five, belonging to Lady Hao, dated to 1250 BCE. She was buried with her servants. Bronze vessels for holding wine or meat were unearthed inscribed with the Lady Hao's name. She was the wife of King Wu (c. 1200 BCE.) From the inscriptions we know that the king made divinations about her illness and pregnancies, and Lady Hao was in charge of some rituals in the court. The tomb was filled with extraordinary sacrificial goods including 460 bronze objects, 750 jades, 70 stone sculptures, 500 hairpins, and 6900 cowrie shells.

Chinese Characters

Character	Seal script	Clerical script	Semi-cursive script	Cursive script	Traditional script	Simplified script
Bird	鳥	烏	鳥	鸟	鸟	鳥
Chinese dragon	龍	龍	龍	龙	龍	龙
Chinese phoenix	鳳	鳳	鳳	凤	鳳	凤
Eye	目	目	目	目	目	
Horse	馬	馬	馬	马	馬	马
Human	人	人	人	人	人	
Moon	月	月	月	月	月	
Mother	母	母	母	母	母	
Mountain	山	山	山	山	山	
Ox	牛	牛	牛	牛	牛	
Rain	雨	雨	雨	雨	雨	
Rice plant	禾	禾	禾	禾	禾	
Sheep	羊	羊	羊	羊	羊	
Sun	日	日	日	日	日	
Tortoise	龜	龜	龜	龟	龜	龜
Water	水	水	水	水	水	
Woman	女	女	女	女	女	
Wood	木	木	木	木	木	

The City of Anyang

Full-scale excavations began at Anyang in 1928 and a major capital city of the Shang Dynasty was revealed in the ensuing decades. Archaeologists have unearthed extensive architectural foundations, tombs, chariots, thousands of bronze vessels, almost uncountable ceramics, and about 150,000 oracle bones.

The excavation sites at Anyang include the remains of over 50 stamped-earth foundations of temples and palaces, the largest of which measures around 230 by 130 feet (70 by 40 meters). Residential and workshop areas within the city contain evidence of carving – particularly of jade – bronze-casting, pottery-making, and bone-working.

Oracle bones

Shang kings communicated with their ancestors through divination or rituals. Archaeological discoveries brought to light the so-called "oracle bones," with long inscriptions about sacrificial offerings, the king's toothache, or the outcome of a war. The diviner applied a glowing metal poker or open fire to turtle shells or cattle shinbones. The resulting heat-cracks were interpreted as signs of good or bad omen.

The Zhou Dynasty (1100–256 BCE)

The Zhou Dynasty inherited and built on the ways and traditions of the earlier Neolithic and Shang cultures – they defeated the Shang in a battle in 1050 BCE. The early Zhou period is the first in which written texts are exchanged, mostly on bamboo slips bound together like small booklets. It was also the time of great changes in ideas about life and death.

Human sacrifices were replaced by effigies made out of wood or stone. Divination declined and the concept of heaven subordinating earthly rulers who mediated between heaven and earth, was introduced. Intellectual concepts were established during the seventh through to the third centuries. Confucianism and Daoism were the main philosophical approaches during this time. The period also saw the decline of the royal Zhou house and the rise of territorial kings, culminating in the defeat of the Zhou.

The Bells of Marquis Yi of the State of Zeng

Bells have played an important role as musical instruments in religious and mourning ceremonies of the Chinese people for more then 3,000 years. A remarkable set of 65 bells was discovered in the tomb of Marquis Yi of the old state of Zeng (in today's Hubei Province.) Inscriptions on the bells date the find to 433 BCE.

The bells make up a very impressive 125 musical instruments with a large set of chime bells. The oval-shaped bells were hung in three tiers from a wooden bell rack. They were struck from the outside by wooden poles and sticks. Each bell produced two tones, when the musicians struck the front or the side of the bell. Together with several other instruments such as stone chimes, drums, zither, and *sheng* pipes, the chime bells were part of a huge orchestra.

LEFT Ancient Chinese bell.

Confucius

The earliest of the Chinese philosophers was Confucius (551–479 BCE.) He was born in Lu, a small state in today's Shandong province, and had been the fief of a duke of Zhou. In Confucius' vision, filial piety, the respect of children for their parents, was essential. This was also true for society, which was seen as a large-scale family. The highest virtue was *ren*: perfect goodness, humanity, and nobility, a virtue without the hierarchical dimension of filial piety. Confucius's thoughts were primarily recorded by his disciples in the *Analects* (*Lunyu*.) The *Analects* provide the foundation for much of Chinese social, political, and ethical thought.

Silk

Native to northern China, the silkworm is the larva of a moth, whose diet consists solely of mulberry leaves. The silkworm is so

ABOVE The Great Wall of China.

called because it spins its cocoon from raw silk. The cocoon is made of a single continuous thread of raw silk, whose length varies from 980 to 3000 feet (300 to 900 m.) To get a long thread, silkworm cocoons are thrown into boiling water, which kills them and also makes the cocoons easier to unravel. Archaeological remains reveal that the Shang were already making silk textiles. By the fourth century BCE, damasks and silk embroideries were in fashion.

Mashan

In 1982, the remains of a 40- or 45- year-old woman were discovered in a small wooden-chambered tomb at Mashan, Hubei Province. She was wearing several layers of garments, and additionally was wrapped in several layers of textiles. Astonishingly, these textiles were so well preserved that they could be unfolded and taken from the dead body.

On opening the coffin lid, the archaeologists found a silk robe on top made of plain-weave silk and a silk quilt with embroidered dragon and phoenix patterns. The body was underneath these and the face was covered with a trapezoidal handkerchief. Hands and feet (with shoes on) were tied together with a silk ribbon, and the hands held a longish object to keep the fingers from bending. The body itself was wrapped in garments and quilts tied tightly with nine ribbons. In total, the lady was wrapped in 19 pieces of clothing and quilts including brocade quilts, a lined quilt, eight brocade robes, three unlined robes, one lined robe, two unlined skirts, and a pair of brocade trousers.

FACT

From the seventh to fourth centuries, two revolutionary improvements in farming technology took place. The first was the development of water-conservation projects. The second was the use of iron tools and invention of the plow.

The Qin Dynasty (221–206 BCE)

After a long period of the so-called Warring States, the First Emperor of China, Qin Shi Huangdi (221–206 BCE), unified China. He standardized weights, the writing system, administration, and currency. His large tomb with its Terracotta Army indicates his military power and his concern for the afterlife.

Qin Shi Huangdi also built what we know today as the Great Wall of China. This project started as regional, separate military fortifications against intrusion by tribes from the north and west on the borders during the seventh century BCE. Under the government of Qin Shi Huangdi the separate walls were connected to form a defensive system on the northern border of the country. It took about 10 years to finish the construction. With an average height of 33 feet (10 m) and width of 16 feet (5 m), the wall runs up and down along the mountain ridges and valleys from east to west. The total length reaches 12,700 li – over 3000 miles (5000 km). The present Great Wall near Beijing mainly dates from the Ming Dynasty (1368–1644 CE).

The Tomb of the First Emperor

As soon as the First Emperor ascended the throne, works began for his necropolis at the Li mountain, close to today's city of Xi'an, Shaanxi province. It required 700,000 slaves to finish the large tomb. The *Records of the Historian*, written by court writer Sima Qian (145–86 BCE), records that the tomb chamber was furnished with thousands of precious grave goods, and it was built with mountains and rivers, and a depiction of the celestial constellations, representing a colorful microcosm of the Universe. Excavations in the last 30 years have shown that this micro-cosmos extended beyond the tomb itself. Three large pits filled with life-sized terracotta soldiers guarded the tomb. However, soon after the completion of the necropolis, it was plundered by the troops of the emperor of the later Han Dynasty. Burning, destruction of the tomb pits, and plundering of the precious weapons ruined the whole structure and also the wonderful coloring of the terracotta figures. The majority of the soldiers have lost their coloring, but traces of the wonderful painting are still visible.

Terracotta Army

What is so remarkable about the terracotta figures is that they are life-sized models but each one has individual characteristics, varying in height, uniform, and hairstyle in accordance with rank. The statues of the infantry soldiers range between 5 foot 8 inches (1.7 m) and 6 foot 2 inches (1.9 m) while the commanders are 6 and a half feet (2 m) tall. It is believed that they were manufactured by government laborers and local craftsmen, and were originally painted in vivid colors with molded faces and real weapons and armor. However, their existence serves as a testament to the amount of labor and skill involved in their construction. It is also proof of the incredible amount of power the First Emperor possessed to order such a monumental undertaking as the manufacturing of the Terracotta Army.

LEFT A Terracotta Army statue from the tomb of the First Emperor.

Han Dynasty (206 BCE–220 CE)

The Han Dynasty asserted sovereignty over vast regions of today's China with a policy of continuous expansion. It was also the beginning of extensive trade with foreigners along the Silk Road. On a technical level, agriculture advanced during the Han Dynasty. Methods of planting two crops in alternation and the use of oxen to draw plows improved the agriculture system. Arts and crafts were produced for the Emperor in special imperial manufacturing workshops. The hope for immortality found expression in large tombs with precious lacquer and silk grave goods.

The tomb of Mawangdui

Scientific excavation of the tomb of Mawangdui, in the city of Changsha, Hunan province, started in April 1972 with tomb number one. The tomb contained the remarkably well-preserved corpse of a lady, who had died in her 50s, and more than 1000 grave goods. Tombs number two and three were discovered in 1973, and made the identification and the exact dating of all three graves possible through the inscriptions on seals and bamboo strips. Tomb number two belonged to Li Cang, prime minister of the king of Changsha, who received tribute from the little state of Dai. He died in 186 BCE. His son, buried in tomb three, died almost 20 years later in 168 BCE, aged 30 years. Tomb one remained intact and untouched, and could be attributed to Xin Zhui, the wife of Li Cang and mother of the owner of tomb number three.

Besides precious lacquers, textiles, and bronzes, 48 bamboo cases with lids, tied with hemp cords, were discovered. Some had clay seals and wooden tags indicating the contents, inscribed "Majordomo of the household of Marquis Dai;" six contained garments and silk fabrics; 30 held foodstuffs, such as grains like rice, wheat, oat, millet, soya beans, red lentils, hemp seeds, pears, plums, arbutus, jujubes, mustard greens, ginger, and lotus root, as well as bones from animals such as ox, sheep, pig, deer, dog, hare, crane, wild goose, duck, pheasant, chicken, sparrow, and carp.

The Six Dynasties (220–581 CE)

China was fragmented for more then three centuries after the fall of the Han. Short-lived courts were the norm, and none of the smaller states gained control over the entire territory of China. A new religious influence arrived in China along with commercial goods, along the Silk Road. The landscape of China was transformed by Buddhism as temples and monasteries were built in towns and remote areas. Large cave temples, such as Dunhuang and Mogao, were drilled into the mountain ranges.

FACT

Buddhism had an enormous impact on visual art in China, especially on sculpture and painting. The most extensive surviving early Chinese Buddhist art is found in cave temples such as Yungang and Dunhuang. The huge Buddha at Yungang is approxiamtely 490 feet (150 m) tall and some 51,000 Buddhist images were carved into the rocks.

Acrobatic art

Chinese acrobatic art began in the fifth century BCE, but it took another 200 years to develop into the so-called "Hundred Plays," an acrobatic show with music. The acrobatic shows developed from farmers who, to while away the wintertime, started to entertain themselves with juggling, tumbling, and balancing. A stone engraving found in a Han tomb in Yinan, Shandong province, provides a vivid picture of acrobats performing in a circus, showing ball-juggling, "tightrope walking over a mountain of knives," hoop-diving, and balancing acts on long poles – these were the most popular shows at this time. In other tombs, archaeologists found small clay figurines of groups of acrobats posing in handstands and a muscular man beating a round drum.

Chinese Dynasties

Era	Date
Prehistoric Times	(1.7 million years–the 21st century BCE)
Xia Dynasty	(21st–16th century BCE)
Shang Dynasty	(16th–11th century BCE)
Zhou Dynasty	
Western Zhou	(11th century BCE–771 BCE)
Eastern Zhou	— Spring and Autumn Period (770 BCE–476 BCE)
	— Warring States Period (403 BCE–256 BCE)
Qin Dynasty	(221 BCE–206 BCE)
Han Dynasty	
Western Han	(206 BCE–24 CE)
Eastern Han	(25–220 CE)
Three Kingdoms Period	(220–265 CE)
Jin Dynasty	
Western Jin	(265–316 CE)
Eastern Jin	(317–420 CE)
Northern and Southern Dynasties	
Northern Dynasties	(386–581 CE)
Southern Dynasties	(420–589 CE)
Sui Dynasty	(589–618 CE)

FACT

Surgical operations on the brain may have been in use in China nearly 3,000 years ago. In the northwestern region of Xinjiang, 13 perforated skulls have been found, bearing between one to five holes each. The healing tissue suggests they were made while the people were still alive.

AFRICA

Changing ways of life

Five thousand years ago, the peoples of the vast continent of Africa lived in diverse ways in different areas and environments. Over time, hunting and gathering – the way of life of our oldest ancestors – was supplemented by stock-herding and later by agriculture. However, the older ways persisted in adapted forms in many areas, even into modern times. The origins of settled living lie in the southern Sahara, about 8,000 BCE. Hunter-fisher-gatherers had adopted agriculture well before 3,000 BCE in pre-Dynastic Egypt. Cattle and stock herding and crop cultivation were adopted later in western, central, and sub-Saharan Africa. Sedentary living and the acquisition of iron technology led to large settlements and extensive trans- and intercontinental trade. By the second millennium BCE, powerful, wealthy states and complex societies had emerged in western, central, and southern Africa.

Northeast Africa

Northeast Africa includes what we now know as Sudan and Ethiopia. Major cities developed in this area, the remains of which can still be seen today.

Timeline

3000 – 2700 BCE
Archaic Period
(Egypt)

2500 BCE
Desertification
of the Sahara
region

770 BCE
Kushites conquer
Egypt (25th Dynasty)

c. 300 BCE
Kushite kingdom
of Meroe
established

3rd millennium BCE
First Kushite kingdom:
Kerma

2000 BCE
Spread of
cattle-keeping in
West Africa

c. 500 BCE
Early iron
technology in
Nigeria and Niger

c. BCE 300–250 CE
Jenne-Jeno (Mali):
rise of urban centers

FACT

"With the possible exception of the Egyptian Nile Valley, no part of Africa saw the rise of a wholly indigenous literate civilization… . It may be argued, at least in part, that it was the richness of the African environment and its lack of physical barriers which permitted many African societies to develop their own forms and orders without the constraints imposed by literate civilization." D. Phillipson.

Kush

Kush was the Egyptian name for Upper and Lower Nubia, south of the city of Aswan in Sudan. Kerma, the first Kushite capital, was established in the third millennium BCE. It became a powerful center, with an elite mud-brick castle (the Western Defuffa) and extensive cemeteries. It declined after conquest by the Egyptians in about 1500 BCE, but regained independence 500 years later. In 770 BCE, the Kushites seized power in Egypt, establishing the 25th Dynasty before being conquered in turn by the Assyrians in 671 BCE. A short-lived civic center was established at Napata, on the Fourth Cataract of the River Nile, before the capital was re-established at Meroe.

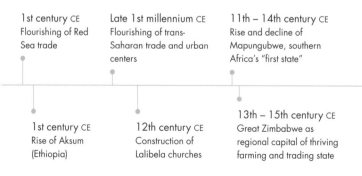

1st century CE
Flourishing of Red
Sea trade

Late 1st millennium CE
Flourishing of trans-
Saharan trade and urban
centers

11th – 14th century CE
Rise and decline of
Mapungubwe, southern
Africa's "first state"

1st century CE
Rise of Aksum
(Ethiopia)

12th century CE
Construction of
Lalibela churches

13th – 15th century CE
Great Zimbabwe as
regional capital of thriving
farming and trading state

Meroe

Meroe, on the Nile's east bank, covered about 1 square mile (2.5 km².)
A walled enclosure contained a royal quarter, temples, government
buildings, and bath areas, with separate aristocratic and commoners'
cemeteries on the periphery. The economy was based on cattle,
sorghum and millet cultivation, iron production, and extensive
Red Sea trade. Small pyramids marked graves of the elite, some
buried with fine goods, servants, and animals. Egyptian religious and
cultural influences are evident in the architecture, but the Meroitic
language and script – still incompletely deciphered – later dominated
on public buildings and stelae (carved pillars.) The settlement
declined in the first centuries CE, possibly for environmental reasons
or because of the rise of Aksum, which conquered Meroe in the
fourth century CE.

FACT

The Periplus of the Erythraean Sea is an anonymous Greek
document of c. 40–70 CE that describes early Red Sea
trade and east coast trading centers. It is important because
archaeological evidence for early trade is scanty.

Aksum

The Ethiopian city of Aksum rose in the first century CE and
survived for about 600 years. Southern Arabian immigrants had
settled there perhaps seven centuries earlier and Aksumite culture
and religion blended Asian and indigenous elements. Under Ezana,
Aksum converted to Christianity in the fourth century CE. The
Aksumites kept cattle, sheep, and goats and cultivated barley, wheat,
and teff. The minting of their own coins indicates the economic
importance of trade. After Meroe's decline, Aksum controlled Red
Sea trade through the port of Adulis. Exported local goods included
animal products (skins, ivory, tortoiseshell), gemstones, and slaves.
Iron was locally available and glass and textiles were locally made, but

fine glassware, cloth, and metal goods were imported. Such items were found during excavation of the Tomb of the Brick Arches. Pre-Christian architecture in Aksum is notable for its multi-storey buildings (perhaps palaces) and funerary stelae, whose design echoes the multi-storey structures. Coinage and altars reflected Christianization. Aksum and its satellite centers declined in the seventh century CE after the Arabs gained control of Red Sea trade.

The Renders Ruin Hoard (found Great Zimbabwe, 1903): the goods of a Swahili trader	
Glass beads	Gold beads
Brass wire	Iron tools
Gold wire	Cowrie shells

Lalibela

The rock-hewn churches of Lalibela in Ethiopia are cut from the Lasta mountains. They are made to look like buildings but technically are "sculpted." Some are free-standing, completely detached from the mountainside. The site dates initially to the seventh and eighth century CE, the time of Aksum's decline. The oldest churches may have originally been palaces or fortified residences. Later churches date to the twelfth and early thirteenth centuries CE, when King Lalibela of the Zagwe Dynasty had a legendary vision that prompted him to create a "new Jerusalem." Some architectural details refer to Aksum, with one church a replica of an Aksumite palace. The Zagwe dynasty was overthrown around 1270 CE.

RIGHT Many churches of Lalibela take their name and layout from features and places in Jerusalem.

Indigenous plants domesticated by African peoples

West and central Africa	Ethiopian region
Yams (various types)	Teff (cereal)
Guinea rice (cereal)	Noog (oil-yielding herb)
Cow peas (pulse)	Enset (banana-like plant)
Groundnuts	Finger millet (cereal)
Sorghum (cereal)	
Bulrush millet (cereal)	
Fonio (cereal)	

West and Central Africa

Dates for stock herding and crop cultivation in western Africa suggest a shift from hunting and fishing much later than in the northeast, around 2000 BCE. Crop cultivation may have begun earlier, but plant remains survive poorly. Mounds 4000 years old excavated at Karkarichinkat, Mali, show that hunting and fishing, but not crop cultivation, supplemented cattle-keeping at that time. Clay figurines of cattle indicate the social importance of this economic innovation. Research in Central Africa suggests that arboriculture (cultivation of tree foods) including early banana cultivation occurred there.

FACT

Indigenous domesticated plants include sorghum, millet, and African rice. The cereals, finger millet and teff, the banana-like enset, and oil-rich noog were particular to Ethiopia. West Africa provided groundnuts, cowpeas, and various types of yam.

Jenne-Jeno

In about 250 BCE Jenne-Jeno, in the Niger Delta in Mali, was a village settled by farming peoples familiar with iron technology. By 300 CE it was a 62-acre (25 hectare) walled settlement, with smaller settlements around it. Its inhabitants cultivated millet, sorghum, and African rice, herded cattle, hunted, and fished. Jenne-Jeno's growth probably developed from trading food surpluses for metals, including imported gold items. Terracotta figurines of domestic and wild animals were present in older levels and later, terracotta heads. The town flourished throughout the first millennium CE, with the population reaching perhaps 10,000. The Jenne-Jeno people included specialized potters and smiths. Despite affluence and a division of labor, social stratification – with an elite controlling wealth – does not seem to have arisen. Jenne-Jeno's decline is poorly understood, but by the mid-second millennium CE a neighboring Islamic town had become the region's economic center.

Metallurgy and economy

Copper and ironworking technology were introduced to Egypt from Asia, and to North Africa by the eighth century BCE, perhaps by the Phoenicians. Debates continue about dating, and whether metallurgy elsewhere in Africa was independently invented. Early copper-working and mining in Mauretania dates to between the eighth and third centuries BCE. Early dates for iron-working in western regions come from mid-first millennium BCE sites in Nigeria and Niger. The spread of iron-working technology throughout the subcontinent is linked to a rapid dispersal of Bantu-speaking agropastoralist peoples, from about 2500 years ago, according to evidence from East Africa. These sites are assigned to the "Chifumbaze complex" ("Early Iron Age.") The beginning of the "Later Iron Age," arbitrarily set at around 1000 CE, corresponds to the rise of states.

FACT
The oldest evidence for knowledge of iron technology in the subcontinent is from Katuruka in Tanzania, around 2300 years ago.

Metallurgy in West African urban centers

Nok *The earliest West African evidence for iron-working comes from the Nigerian village of Nok. Mining uncovered fragments of terracotta figures, mainly of humans – the oldest African sculptural tradition outside Egypt. Furnaces, iron slag, and associated Nok tradition sites have since been dated to between the fifth and third centuries BCE. Iron was used to make knives and spearpoints. The terracottas, which range from 4 inches (10 cm) tall to nearly life-size, are highly distinctive in style. Some may have been placed on shrines. Nok endured until the second century CE.*

Ife *Ife is another Nigerian urban center that has yielded terracotta sculptures, dating to the end of the first millennium CE. Notable, but less abundant, are brass heads, made using the "lost wax" technique. Sparse evidence for the site's early history suggests that Ife's economy was based on yam cultivation and extensive trade, importing glass beads and copper. Buildings were probably of sun-dried mud. The city was laid out with pavements unusually edged with upright potsherds.*

Benin *This city was contemporary with Ife in the West African forest region. Benin had a population of perhaps 10,000 people by the fifteenth century. Its celebrated brass sculptures, dating to the city's later history, include figures of the ruling elite. From about 1000 CE, vast earthworks covering thousands of square miles ringed the city and subdivided surrounding areas.*

Rock art

The hunter–gatherer ancestors of the San people (or "Bushmen") of sub-Saharan Africa are the continent's oldest original inhabitants. Their rock art is particularly celebrated. Areas rich in rock paintings include the South African Drakensberg and Cederberg ranges, the Brandberg in Namibia, the Matopos in Zimbabwe, and parts of Tanzania. Hunter-gatherers were making images at least 10,000 years ago, with figures on cave and shelter walls produced from at least 3,600 years ago. The principal subjects were people and animals, especially large herbivores. Abundant images of the eland, the largest antelope, important in San mythology, provide clues to the religious motivation of the artists. Petroglyphs, or rock carvings, occur in more arid areas of southern Africa.

Abundant rock paintings and petroglyphs found in the Sahara Desert are evidence of a wetter climate, when both animals and people congregated by lakes and rivers. Some images of wild animals

ABOVE A panel from Game Pass, one of South Africa's most important rock art sites, depicting eland and part-human, part-animal figures.

Human-made landscapes

Earthworks: ditch and rampart structures	
Eredo	In the Nigerian swampland, tenth totwelfth century CE earthworks ; thought to have had monumental and religious significance, rather than serving a defensive function.
Benin, Udo	Southern Nigerian earthworks, 10,000 miles (16,000 km) long, ringed and subdivided the large urban settlements of the early to middle second millennium CE.
Bigo	Capital of one of the Central African "interlacustrine kingdoms" in present-day Uganda, ringed and internally subdivided by earthworks dating from around the fourteenth century, which extended over 3.8 square miles (10 km²).
Ntusi	In the Central African "interlacustrine kingdoms," sites with earthworks, interpreted as ancient dams.
Agricultural terraces	
Engaruka (Tanzania)	On the slopes of Mount Ngorongoro, extensive stone terraces for irrigation of crops, and hillside gardens, mid-second millenium.
Nyanga (Zimbabwe)	Extensive mountainside stone terraces for irrigation, mid-second millennium CE.

may predate pastoralism, but many images of people and their cattle were made by herders. In the later art, horses, horse-drawn chariots, and camels were depicted. Increasing aridity, leading to desertification, set in about 2500 BCE.

African rock art has been subject to many interpretations and wrongly attributed to foreign peoples including Phoenicians and Indian immigrants. Ample evidence connects much rock art to mythology and religious practises. Some believe that rock art, especially in southern Africa, depicts shamans' hallucinatory visions. However, while connections to religious practise and mythological beings are often clear, there is little to connect many, perhaps most, images with shamanic rituals rather than mythology or a wider spectrum of religious practises.

Trade

From the later first millennium CE the Sahara Desert was criss-crossed by important trade routes, linking West African states to North Africa and beyond. Twelfth-century tombstones at Gao, capital of the Songhai empire, were apparently imported from Spain. The most important trade product carried by camel caravan across the desert was West African gold, exchanged for salt. Slaves, metals, and cowrie shells were among other trade items.

Timbuktu

The legendary city of Timbuktu, in the Songhai kingdom, prospered on trans-Saharan trade. Founded around 900 CE, it was a wealthy Islamic city, with a university famous throughout the medieval world.

ABOVE Timbuktu, in Mali, was a spiritual and intellectual capital in the fifteenth and sixteenth centuries.

World contact: Exotic goods in Later Iron Age sites subcontinental Africa

Artifact	Place of origin
Pottery	China, Persia
Glass	Near East
Cowrie shells	East Africa
Cloth	Asia
Glass beads	Arikamedu, India; Fustat, Egypt; "Indo-Pacific" beads: southeast Asia, Malaysia and environs

The rise of southern African states

The site of Mapungubwe, in northeastern South Africa, marks the rise of states and complex societies in the subcontinent in the early second millennium CE.

Mapungubwe

A thriving center, with a population that reached perhaps 5,000, Mapungubwe marks the emergence of social stratification in the region. A hilltop-dwelling elite were buried with rich grave goods. The settlement was linked to Indian Ocean trade, with gold, ivory, and other products traded for glass beads, cloth, and exotic goods. The center declined by the fourteenth century, with economic power passing to Great Zimbabwe to the north.

FACT

An island off the Kenyan coast, Kilwa Kisiwani began as a small Islamic town. Prosperous centers rose across Africa at the end of the first millennium CE and Kilwa became important in intercontinental trade, flourishing under the thirteenth-century Shirazi dynasty.

Great Zimbabwe

Great Zimbabwe, subject of much myth-making about "lost" cities and exotic immigrants, was the center of a large state with many smaller *dzimbabwes* in surrounding areas. Its distinctive dry-stone walling probably postdates initial settlement in the late thirteenth century. Walls seems to have connected and defined activity-areas and symbolic spaces used by the ruling elite, rather than serving defensive purposes. A solid dry-stone conical tower dominates the Great Enclosure. Celebrated finds are six carved soapstone birds, designed for mounting on pillars. The center flourished on east coast and intercontinental trade, with gold being a lucrative export. Imports included glass beads and oriental porcelain.

The domestic economy of Great Zimbabwe was founded on cattle-keeping. At its height, the population reached perhaps 18,000.

ABOVE A view of the Great Enclosure at Great Zimbabwe, showing the Conical Tower.

Environmental pressure may have prompted its late fifteenth-century decline. Other possibilities include a new demand for copper from centers to the north, and political factors. Successor settlements endured until the nineteenth century.

FACT

Great Zimbabwe Tradition is the name for a series of southern African Later Iron Age settlements, dating from the early second millennium CE to recent times. The Shona word *dzimbabwe* means "stone house" or "venerated house."

Notable African artefacts and artworks

Artifact	Description
Afro Ayigeba	A richly decorated brass cross dating to the eleventh century CE. Stolen from the church of Bet Medhane Alem at Lalibela, Ethiopia; returned in 2001.
Aksum stela	Looted by Mussolini in 1937 from Aksum and erected in Rome; returned to Ethiopia in 2005.
Benin bronzes	"Bronze" (actually brass) sculptures; accomplished workmanship, made using the "lost wax" technique, much sought after by antiquities collectors.
Wadi Sura	An area in the Libyan desert with rock paintings that inspired those depicted in the "Cave of Swimmers," featured in the film *The English Patient*.
White Lady of the Brandberg	Room painting in Namibia's Tsisab Ravine, Brandberg mountains, discovered by a surveyor in 1917. Initially interpreted as in an "Egyptian-Mediterranean"style and as evidence of foreign influence, the composition is now known to depict a male figure, and to be the work of San artists.
Zimbabwe birds	Six soapstone carvings of birds, designed to stand on pillars, found at Great Zimbabwe; probably symbols of elite authority.

BRONZE AGE
AEGEAN

Aegean setting

The Aegean is flanked by mainland Greece to the west and Turkey to the east; its northern limit is marked by Macedonia and Thrace, and to the south is the island of Crete. Two key cultural groups in the Late Bronze Age are known from Crete and mainland Greece.

Thera

The island of Thera lies in the southern Aegean, 70 miles (110 kilometers) to the north of Crete. At the start of the Late Bronze Age there was a massive volcanic eruption which buried the small town at Akrotiri. Some of the buildings were several storeys tall, and their interiors were decorated with elaborate frescoes. These include a scene that shows women collecting crocus flowers and presenting their offerings to a seated female figure, who is likely to be a deity.

Mycenae

The discovery of gold funerary goods, including masks from Shaft Grave Circle A, appears to confirm the wealth of Mycenae that is reflected in the Homeric poems, such as *The Iliad*. These burials date from the late seventeenth century BCE. The upper city was contained

Timeline

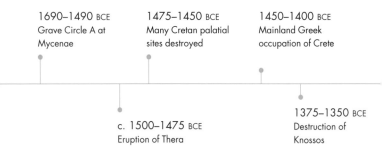

1690–1490 BCE	1475–1450 BCE	1450–1400 BCE
Grave Circle A at Mycenae	Many Cretan palatial sites destroyed	Mainland Greek occupation of Crete

c. 1500–1475 BCE
Eruption of Thera

1375–1350 BCE
Destruction of Knossos

by a substantial stone wall constructed during the Late Bronze Age. It was entered through a monumental gate which was surmounted by two lions. The citadel contained a palace (or *megaron*) decorated with murals.

ABOVE Grave Circle A, Mycenae, c. 1600–1400 BCE.

1370–1300 BCE
Fortification walls built
at Mycaenae

c. 1200 BCE
Destruction of
Mycenae

After 1305 BC
The Ulu Burun
shipwreck

c. 1100 BCE
End of the
Bronze Age

Palatial civilization

Palatial centers first emerged in Crete. They varied in form over time and had economic, social, and political functions.

Palace at Knossos

At least four palaces are known from Crete in the Middle to Late Bronze Age: Phaistos on the Mesara plain in the south, Knossos in the center, Malia on the north coast, and Kato Zakro in the east. Knossos was the largest of these, which suggests that it was the primary palace on the island. One of the main features of the Cretan palaces was a large, open central courtyard. This was surrounded by domestic quarters, storage areas, and rooms set aside for cults. The rooms of the palace were decorated with frescoes.

Pylos

The palace of Pylos lies in the western Peloponnese. A complex palace structure has been discovered dating to the Late Bronze Age. During the destruction of the palace, around 1200 BCE, the clay tablets in the palace archive just inside the entrance were baked hard, preserving their text. These tablets show the extent of the territories that relate to the palace.

Linear B

The remains of small clay tablets, scored with lines framing what appeared to be pictograms, were found in the Late Bronze Age palaces of Crete and mainland Greece. The form of writing, known as Linear B, was shown to be an early form of Greek. The tablets provide information about the economy of the palaces and about crops and workers.

Egypt and the Aegean

A series of faience plaques bearing the cartouche of the 18th Dynasty Egyptian pharaoh Amenhotep III have been found at several locations at Mycenae. Scarabs relating to the same pharaoh have been found on Crete and at other sites in mainland Greece. A statue base from Kom el–Hetan, the mortuary temple of Amenhotep III in western Thebes, appears to list a series of Aegean place names, confirming links between Egypt and the Aegean.

Aegean art

Aegean art is set apart by its naturalistic and vivid style which often depicted mythological, symbolic, and ritualistic concepts.

Wall paintings

Fragmentary remains of Minoan-style wall-paintings have been uncovered by excavations at Tel el Dab'a (Avaris) in the eastern Nile Delta; they appear to be associated with an early 18th Dynasty palace established after the fall of the Hyksos capital. Among the wall-paintings is one of a bull-leaping scene, reminiscent of murals from Knossos on Crete.

ABOVE Palace ruins at Knossos, Crete, Greece.

Funerary friezes

Representations of Aegean peoples ("Keftiu") are found in funerary scenes in the elite tombs at Thebes dating to the 18th Dynasty (New Kingdom.) The tomb of the Egyptian vizier Rekhmire contains a frieze of Keftiu apparently bringing gifts to Egypt, including what appear to be copper ingots.

The Ulu Burun shipwreck

A major Late Bronze Age shipwreck has been discovered off the coast of southern Turkey with a date of 1318 BCE suggested by dendrochronology (the study of tree rings to determine dates.) Its cargo was rich in archaeological finds including:

Copper ingots *11 tons (10,000 kg) of copper ingots which chemical analysis have linked to mines on the island of Cyprus.*

Glass ingots *175 blue glass ingots of a type known from Egypt, and hippopotamus ivory.*

Amphoras *150 Cannaanite transport amphoraes which contained terebinth resin, known to have been used in temples in Egypt.*

Gold scarab *Among the smaller finds was a gold scarab with the name of Nefertiti, the wife of Akhenaten.*

Troy

The fortified site at Hissarlik, on the Asian side of the Dardenelles in modern Turkey, has been identified as the site of the Bronze Age city of Troy (or Ilion) which formed the subject of Homer's epic *Iliad*. Excavations have revealed a series of walled cities, some apparently destroyed by fire. The Late Bronze Age cities are known as Troy VI and VII. A geophysical survey has found evidence for a rampart around the lower wall which appears to be contemporary with the Late Bronze Age settlement. Recent excavations have revealed remains of the Roman city, including a portrait of the emperor Augustus.

EUROPE

Agricultural settlement

Prehistoric societies existed in Europe for hundreds of millennia during the Ice Age, but people began to settle down following the establishment of modern environmental conditions around 10,000 years ago. Agriculture appeared in southeastern Europe about 9,000 years ago and spread throughout the continent over the next 3,000 years. Farming settlements were connected by a web of paths, trails, and streams, so people moved among them bringing new ideas and technology.

Megaliths

In northern and western Europe, farmers began to build tombs and monuments from large stones, known as "megaliths."

Megaliths of Carnac

On the coast of Brittany, around the town of Carnac, lies a remarkable collection of prehistoric monuments. Long burial mounds and standing stones called menhirs were built first, around 4000 BCE. The massive mounds were between 400 and 650 feet (120 and 200 meters) long. The menhirs were nearby, including the Grand Menhir Brisé which was over 66 feet (20 meters) tall. Next came passage

Timeline

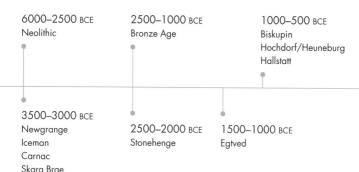

6000–2500 BCE	2500–1000 BCE	1000–500 BCE
Neolithic	Bronze Age	Biskupin
		Hochdorf/Heuneburg
		Hallstatt

3500–3000 BCE	2500–2000 BCE	1500–1000 BCE
Newgrange	Stonehenge	Egtved
Iceman		
Carnac		
Skara Brae		

graves, in which pieces of some of the menhirs were reused when they were built around 3500 BCE. In fact, two pieces of the same menhir were incorporated into different passage graves.

Finally, around 3000 BCE, the inhabitants of the Carnac region began erecting long rows of standing stones. At Le Menec, over 1,000 stones stand in 10 rows that run for three-quarters of a mile (1.200 km), and at Kermario, a similar number of stones stretch for about two-thirds of a mile (1 km) in seven rows. The purpose of the Carnac stones is unknown, but one possibility is that they guided ceremonial processions to stone enclosures in which rituals were conducted.

ABOVE The Carnac stones, one of the most extensive Neolithic menhir collections in the world.

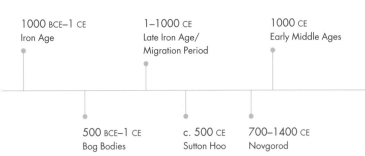

1000 BCE–1 CE
Iron Age

1–1000 CE
Late Iron Age/
Migration Period

1000 CE
Early Middle Ages

500 BCE–1 CE
Bog Bodies

c. 500 CE
Sutton Hoo

700–1400 CE
Novgorod

Stonehenge

Stonehenge, in southern England, is perhaps the most recognizable prehistoric site in Europe, maybe even the world. What tourists see today is only the final Bronze Age stage of the site, from around 2000 BCE. Almost a millennium earlier, Neolithic people had defined the basic outline of the monument with a bank and ditch supplemented by 56 mysterious holes around its perimeter. Around 2500 BCE, stones began to be erected; first a circle of bluestones brought from the Preseli Mountains in Wales, and finally a complex arrangement of Welsh bluestone and local sarsen stones. The sarsen trilithons, in which immense upright stones are capped by equally massive lintels, are the most distinctive architectural element of Stonehenge today. The landscape around Stonehenge contains other monuments and earthworks, as well as hundreds of barrows, or burial mounds.

> **Bush Barrow** *Opened in the early nineteenth century, Bush Barrow held the skeleton of a man accompanied by several objects that testified to his elite status, including a gold belt-hook, a gold breastplate, two bronze daggers, and a bronze ax. Another burial excavated in 2002, 3 miles (5 kilometers) from Stonehenge near Amesbury, contained the skeleton of a man between 35 and 45 years old with gold and copper artifacts,*

ABOVE Stonehenge, in Wiltshire, UK, one of the most famous prehistoric sites in the world.

as well as archer's wristguards made from stone, and flint arrowheads. Tests on the skeleton of the "Amesbury Archer" indicate that he had grown up near the Alps.

Durrington Walls *In 2006, a Neolithic village was discovered at Durrington, about 1¾ miles (3 kilometers) from Stonehenge. Eight rectangular timber houses were excavated, while more are believed to lie buried nearby, and have been dated to 2600 BCE. It seems likely that the people who lived at Durrington were involved with the construction or the use of the monument, given their proximity to Stonehenge. Large quantities of pig bones have been interpreted as the remains of feasting, perhaps connected with ceremonial activities that brought people to the area.*

The Iceman

In 1991, hikers discovered the frozen corpse of a prehistoric man high in the Tyrolean Alps. Since he was discovered near the Ötztal, a glacial valley, he became known in the press as "Ötzi," but a more common name for him is "the Iceman." The Iceman lived and died 5,300 years ago during a period known as the Copper Age. Among his possessions were a copper ax, flint arrowheads, an antler point, containers made from birch bark, a yew bow, and a leather quiver with 14 arrows. A pouch contained mushrooms and a fungus that may have had medicinal properties.

The Iceman wore a bearskin hat, a coat pieced together from goatskin, leggings and a loincloth also made from goatskin, shoes with bearskin soles and deerhide uppers, and a calfskin belt. His most unusual article of clothing was a grass cape that would have been water-repellent and warm. His shoes were also stuffed with grass for insulation.

For nearly twenty years, the Iceman's corpse has been subjected to scientific analysis. We know that he was in his late 40s and stood only about 5 feet 2 inches (1.6 meters) tall. He had suffered broken bones several times in life. His arteries were hardened, he had arthritis, and his lungs were black from inhaling smoke. Some of the

FACT

The Iceman had tattoos on his back, knees, ankles, and left wrist made by rubbing charcoal into small cuts. Perhaps these were not just ornamental but were believed to have a therapeutic effect.

Iceman's toes show signs of frostbite. The Iceman's last meal included wheat and meat, and pollen grains found in his digestive tract indicated that he had died in the late spring.

How did the Iceman die? It was long assumed that he was a traveller who died from exposure or perhaps from a fall while crossing the Alps. In 2001, however, a CAT-scan revealed a small flint arrowhead embedded in his left shoulder. It would have done severe damage to the Iceman's blood vessels and muscles and was probably the cause of his death, especially when coupled with the harsh environment, his other infirmities, and advanced age. We can only speculate about the story surrounding the Iceman's death. Had he been mortally wounded in a raid? Had he been the victim of a feud or an ambush? We may never know why the Iceman was killed. More important is what his body and equipment tell us about how he lived.

Farming and fishing at Skara Brae

The desolate Orkney Islands lie at the edge of the prehistoric European world, but between 3100 and 2500 BCE a remarkable settlement known as Skara Brae housed a community of Neolithic fishers and farmers. Since almost no trees grow on Orkney, the inhabitants of Skara Brae built their houses from slabs of stone in depressions in an old trash dump. Each house had a large central area with a hearth, and some had smaller rooms opening off the main chamber. The houses were interconnected by trenches, roofed with stone. Within the houses, slabs of stone were stacked to

RIGHT Skara Brae, a large stone-built Neolithic settlement on the west coast of mainland Orkney, Scotland, is Europe's most distinctive Neolithic village.

form shelves, while large stone boxes were probably filled with seaweed and covered with furs to make beds.

Burial rituals

Early European peoples developed various burial traditions to safeguard their dead. These included vast monuments with passages that lead to burial chambers, and elaborately decorated and filled coffins.

Burial monuments

Throughout northwestern Europe, Neolithic people built burial monuments from large flat stones set upright to form passages and chambers, which they then roofed over with other large flat stones. Such monuments are known as "passage graves" for they consist of a corridor, or passage, leading into a central burial chamber. Passage graves are known from Spain to Sweden, but those found in Ireland are classic examples of such monuments. Passage graves are found throughout Ireland, but there are four major clusters extending from Sligo in the northwest to the Boyne Valley in the east. At Carrowmore smaller monuments are eclipsed by an

FACT
Stone pits in house floors at Skara Brae were made water-tight with clay and may have been used to store shellfish.

immense passage grave situated on top of Knocknarea mountain, while at Carrowkeel, they are on the peaks themselves. Several hilltops at Lough Crew northwest of Dublin are covered with passage graves.

Newgrange passage grave

The most famous passage grave cemetery in Ireland is found in the Boyne Valley north of Dublin, where the tombs of Knowth, Dowth, and Newgrange were built around 3000 BCE. Newgrange is probably the most famous of these graves. Although its fanciful exterior reconstruction is controversial, its interior passage and chamber are some of the finest passage-grave architecture known. Several stones are engraved with the interlocking spirals that are the hallmark of megalithic art, and the corbelled roof of its main chamber rises to a height of 20 feet (6 meters.) Perhaps the most remarkable detail of Newgrange is that its passage is aligned in such a way that, at dawn on the winter solstice, December 21, the sun shines through a portal over the entrance directly down the passage to illuminate the burial chamber.

Bronze Age Danish coffin burials

The contents of coffins made from hollowed-out tree trunks and buried under layers of turf have revealed details of Bronze Age life in Denmark between 1400 and 1100 BCE. In the coffins were preserved bodies of elite individuals, not just their skeletons but also their hair, nails, and some of their skin. Moreover, their clothing and the hides and blankets that covered them were also preserved. The coffin found at Egtved contained the body of a young woman about 20 years old. She was wearing a woollen tunic and a skirt made from woolen cords rather than cloth. Her long hair was held back by a woolen headband, and on her stomach was a bronze disk about 6 inches (15 centimeters) in diameter. A coffin was lined with cowhide, and a heavy woolen blanket covered the corpse. Sharp-eyed archaeologists noticed a flower between the blanket and the cowhide, which enabled them to determine that the woman had been buried

FACT
Over a 300 year period, during the Bronze Age in Denmark, over 20,000 barrows were constructed.

in the summer. Beside her body was a birchbark vessel that contained traces of a fermented honey beverage.

Hochdorf burial mound

A timber chamber under a mound at Hochdorf in Germany contained the body of a man lying on a bronze sofa. The sofa's eight legs were figures of women with upstretched arms. Nearby was a wagon with four spoked wheels. The walls of the burial chamber were covered with cloth on which nine drinking horns had been hung. The man's clothing and shoes were decorated with bands of gold, and he had a gold ring around his neck. He must have been an elite member of Celtic society between 600 and 500 BCE to receive such an elaborate burial.

Sutton Hoo

Just before World War II, several burial mounds were excavated at Sutton Hoo, in eastern England. In one mound, careful excavation revealed rows of iron rivets, which were known to hold together the planks of ships in the first millennium CE. Archaeologists were able to trace the outlines of the ship in the soil, even though the wood had decayed. This was not just a buried ship, however, but a burial in a ship. The central burial chamber contained an array of objects, including an iron helmet, coat of mail, and sword; textiles including wall hangings and cloaks; a purse with gold ornamentation that held 37 gold coins; drinking horns with silver fittings; 10 silver bowls, and a large silver dish with the stamp of the Byzantine emperor Anastasius. Recent excavations of other mounds have established that this was a cemetery for the Anglo-Saxon elite during the sixth and

Dover Boat

In 1992, road excavations in Dover, England, revealed the remains of a Bronze Age boat that had been abandoned around 1500 BCE. It was over 30 feet (9 meters) long and 8 feet (2.4 meters) wide, estimated to have accommodated 18 or more rowers. The Dover Boat was built by splitting an oak tree into planks, which were then shaped with chisels and adzes, and lashed together with yew wood. Two planks formed the bottom, while four others were used for the sides. The joints were reinforced by strips of oak and packed with moss. The Dover Boat was large enough to have been used to cross the English Channel and provides evidence of travel and trade between Britain and the Continent.

seventh centuries CE, and some of the graves held the remains of the kings of East Anglia.

Spiritual life

The wetlands and bogs that had long had spiritual significance, assumed an even greater role in Iron Age Europe, as the places for sacrifice, not just of objects and animals, but also of humans.

Flag Fen

At the end of the Bronze Age, around 1350 BCE, an immense timber structure was built at Flag Fen near Peterborough, England. Around 80,000 trees were felled to build a wooden alignment of pilings extending for about 3,000 feet (1 kilometer) through a swamp. At the deepest part of the swamp, a large platform was constructed by placing timbers across yet more piles. From this platform, numerous wooden, ceramic, and metal objects were thrown into the swamp as offerings, many deliberately broken. Human and animal bones were also found. The mysterious structure at Flag Fen was maintained for several centuries, until about 950 BCE.

Bog bodies

Across northern Europe, from Ireland to Poland, Iron Age people regarded ponds, springs, and bogs as places with deep spiritual significance. Part of their interaction with the world of their deities was the gruesome sacrifice of men, women, and children, whose bodies were then placed in these wetlands where they have been preserved for over 2,000 years. Such "bog bodies" are frequently found during the digging of peat.

ABOVE The body of Tollund man, a victim of human sacrifice by ritual strangulation.

Lindow Man *He was found in 1984 in England and had been hit over the head and then strangled. For good measure, his throat was slit. One of the most gruesome deaths was suffered by Old Croghan Man, found in 2003 in Ireland, who was stabbed in the chest, decapitated, and subsequently cut in half.*

Tollund Man *Perhaps the most famous bog bodies are those found in the early 1950s in Denmark. Tollund Man was wearing only a belt and a leather cap, but around his neck was the leather cord with which he had been strangled. He was probably in his late 30s and about 5 feet 3 inches (1.6 meters) tall. Contents of his stomach indicated that his last meal was a gruel made from vegetables and grains. Grauballe Man, found two years later, was about 30 when his throat was cut around 300 BCE.*

Clonycavan Man *The find of Clonycavan Man in Ireland in 2003 has provided many new details about Iron Age life. His death was caused by a blow that split open his skull, sometime between 400 and 200 BCE. Clonycavan Man was in his early 20s, only about 5 feet 2 inches (1.6 meters) tall, probably a member of the social elite. Perhaps his most notable attribute was his long hair, which had been elaborately* *styled using a gel made from plant oil and pine resin. Analysis of this gel indicates that it may have come from southern France or Spain, suggesting long-distance trade along the Atlantic coast.*

Commercial centers

In some regions, opportunities for wealth and prestige blossomed with the introduction of metallurgy around 2000 BCE. Traces of these social attributes are found in the burials of the elite under mounds. Commerce and trade led some communities to become very prosperous during the final millennium BCE. Biskupin, Hallstatt, and the Heuneburg in central Europe are examples of such societies.

Hallstatt

At Hallstatt, high in the Austrian Alps, mining of rock salt generated tremendous wealth for its inhabitants between about 700 and 500 BCE. Iron Age miners tunneled along veins of salt, which they shoveled into leather backpacks and carried out of the mountain. Salt was more than just a seasoning; salting was a principal means of preserving meat and fish in prehistoric Europe. It was in such demand that the miners of Hallstatt and their families were able to amass great wealth in return.

This wealth is revealed by the burials in a valley down the slope from the mines. Over 1,000 cremation and skeletal burials have been excavated, while many others either lie undisturbed beneath the mountain soil or have been destroyed by mining operations. Many graves in the Hallstatt cemetery contain objects that were either costly to make or used exotic materials that were difficult to acquire. One sword handle, for example, is made from ivory (which must have come from Africa), inlaid with amber (which must have come from the Baltic coast), and may have been manufactured in Italy. Bronze and iron weapons, bronze bowls and cauldrons, helmets, and ornaments were found in profusion.

Biskupin

Along Lake Biskupin in western Poland, a soggy peninsula yielded the remains of a wooden Iron Age settlement. There were 13 rows of timber houses, separated by streets made from logs, each consisting of an antechamber that led into a central room with a hearth and sleeping quarters. A strong rampart made from timber boxes filled with earth and stones protected the settlement. Wooden stakes between the rampart and the water's edge formed a breakwater to prevent it from being undermined by wave erosion. From tree-ring dating, it is thought that most of the trees used in building the settlement were cut between 747 and 722 BCE, and almost half of them were cut during the winter of 738–737 BCE. An estimated 700–1,000 people lived at Biskupin, most of them farmers who grew millet, wheat, barley, rye, and beans on surrounding fields, and kept pigs for meat and cattle for milk.

FACT

The Heuneburg, a hillfort built around 650 BCE in southwest Germany, had a wall made with sun-dried mudbrick, showing that the chief who lived there had contacts with the Mediterranean world.

Towns and kingdoms

During the first millennium CE chronicles and other texts began to be produced, some of which survive today. They recount the emergence of kings and towns that would be recognizable from early historical accounts.

Staraya Ladoga/Novgorod

The Volkhov River is a vital link in the inland water route between the Baltic and Black Seas that was pioneered by Scandinavian merchants in the eigthth, ninth, and tenth centuries CE. Along the Volkhov, Viking merchants who traded with the Slavs established a series of settlements. Two major trading towns sprang up during this period, Staraya Ladoga downstream and Novgorod upstream. Staraya Ladoga traces its founding to 753 CE. Around this time, another settlement was established upstream near the site of modern Novgorod. Over the next century, the settlements along the Volkhov had populations composed of both Scandinavians and Slavs.

In 862 CE, the Viking prince Rurik arrived in the region and made Staraya Ladoga his capital, which flourished due to trade between Scandinavia and the Near East. Most of the ninth-century Arab coins found in Scandinavia probably passed through Staraya Ladoga. Rurik's successors eventually moved their capital to Novgorod, which developed into a large town with wooden houses and workshops along timber-paved streets. In one location, nearly 30 levels of timber paving were found, dating from the tenth to the fifteenth century CE. Some of the most unusual finds at Novgorod, preserved in the waterlogged sediments, are manuscripts inscribed on birch bark that deal with business, legal, and personal matters.

ABOVE Biskupin, an archaeological site of an Iron Age fortified settlement in Poland, along Lake Biskupin.

CLASSICAL
CIVILIZATION

Classical period

Classical civilization refers to the history and culture of the lands centered around the Mediterranean. Chronologically it stretches roughly from the earliest Greek poetry of Homer in the seventh century BCE through to the fall of the Roman empire in the fifth century CE. It can be divided into the Archaic Greek period, which continues up to the defeat of Athens in the fifth century BCE, the Macedonian and Hellenistic world to the battle of Actium in 133 BCE, and the Roman world, beginning in the eighth century BCE and continuing to the final disintegration in Late Antiquity.

Archaic and Classical Greece

Greece was transformed during the eighth century BCE with the emergence of individual city-states or *poleis*. These units, consisting of an urban community and its surrounding territory, continued into the Roman period. Although they shared a broadly common language and culture, there were individual differences, such as the form of letters in the alphabet. Different political systems emerged in this period, ranging from kings in cities such as Sparta, to tyrannies like the Kypselid family at Corinth, to democracy which emerged at Athens after a period of tyranny. The core Greek cities of the Aegean

Archaic and Classical Greece timeline

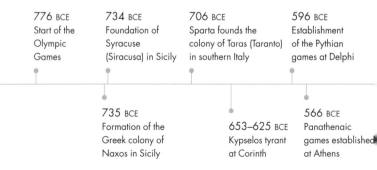

776 BCE
Start of the
Olympic
Games

734 BCE
Foundation of
Syracuse
(Siracusa) in Sicily

706 BCE
Sparta founds the
colony of Taras (Taranto)
in southern Italy

596 BCE
Establishment
of the Pythian
games at Delphi

735 BCE
Formation of the
Greek colony of
Naxos in Sicily

653–625 BCE
Kypselos tyrant
at Corinth

566 BCE
Panathenaic
games established
at Athens

had contact beyond their immediate area, and from the seventh century BCE there was a period of colonizing which took Greek culture to the shores of the Black Sea, to North Africa, and into the south of France and Spain. Greek cities in western Turkey became part of the Persian Empire during the sixth century BCE, which brought the Greeks into conflict with the Persians. This culminated in a major invasion of the Greek mainland in 480–479 and the destruction of Athens. The Greek alliance which repulsed the Persians was transformed into the Delian League, dominated by Athens. Tensions grew between Athens and Sparta, leading to the outbreak of hostilites in 431 known as the Peloponnesian War. This finally ended in 404 BCE with the defeat of Athens.

Sparta

Sparta lay in the valley of the river Eurotas in the southern Peloponnese. Excavations have revealed remains of the sanctuary of Artemis Orthia where finds include objects carved from imported elephant ivory. On the east side of the river lay the Menelaion, where the Spartans worshipped the mythical king Menelaos and his wife Helen. Sparta's conflict with her western neighbor on the other side of the Taygetos mountain range brought about the annexation of Messenia.

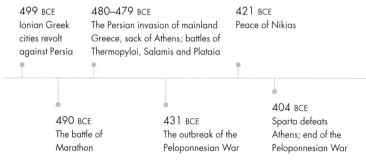

499 BCE
Ionian Greek
cities revolt
against Persia

480–479 BCE
The Persian invasion of mainland
Greece, sack of Athens; battles of
Thermopylai, Salamis and Plataia

421 BCE
Peace of Nikias

490 BCE
The battle of
Marathon

431 BCE
The outbreak of the
Peloponnesian War

404 BCE
Sparta defeats
Athens; end of the
Peloponnesian War

Athens

Athens eventually became the dominant power in the Greek world, as an unchallenged master of the sea and a leading commercial center. Its wealth attracted intellectuals and artists such as Aristophanes, Plato, and Herodotus.

Democracy in Athens: *The roots of democracy, literally "the power of the people" (*demos*), can be traced back to the late seventh century* BCE. *The Athenians were liberated from the tyrant family of the Peisistratids at the end of the sixth century* BCE. *They organized the citizen body into 10 tribes based on the towns and villages of Attica, the area round Athens. One of the key bodies was the* boule *or council which consisted of 50 men from each of the 10 tribes.*

The Athenian Agora: *The political heart of the city of Athens was the agora. Excavations have revealed many of the buildings associated with the democracy, including the law-courts. Finds include water-clocks for timing the length of speeches, as well as simple machines for allotting juries to trials. Inscriptions recording decisions of the political bodies at Athens have also been found. Public accountability is reflected in the complex accounts for building projects and tribute which were "published" on marble stelai.*

The Kerameikos cemetery: *Extensive cemeteries have been discovered clustered outside the gates of the city of Athens. To the north-west, in the area known as the Kerameikos, evidence has been found of public graves that are known from historical texts. Large pits filled with*

FACT

Athenioidans voted to exile prominent citizens by using pot-sherds or *ostraka* written with the name of the candidates. Deposits of such "votes" show that many of the names had been written in the same handwriting, suggesting a possible rigging of the process.

a number of bodies and grave offerings appear to date from the early years of the Peloponnesian War, when the population of Athens was decimated by plague. Marble grave reliefs and free-standing statues were placed on some of the graves in the sixth century BCE; some have been found re-used in the city-walls of Athens.

The Parthenon: *The Parthenon was the main temple of Athena. Dated building accounts for the project show that work started in 447 BCE and was completed in 432. It was part of a major building project in Athens co-ordinated by the Athenian sculptor Pheidias. Roman sources reveal the names of the two architects: Kallikrates, who was also responsible for the small temple of Athena Nike at the western entrance of the Athenian acropolis, and Iktinos, who later designed a temple of Apollo at Bassai in the western Peloponnese. The Parthenon was decorated with a series of sculptures, which included a continuous frieze showing one of the civic processions. Inside was a colossal gold and ivory statue of Athena made by Pheidias; small marble replicas, which were made in the Roman period, have survived.*

ABOVE The Parthenon, a temple of the Greek Goddess Athena built in the fifth century BCE on the Acropolis of Athens.

Theater of Dionysos: *The tragic and comic plays of Athens were performed in the theater of Dionysos on the south slope of the Athenian acropolis. Victorious playwrights were celebrated with monuments, and in the fourth century* BCE *"imaginary" portraits of tragedians such as Euripides were displayed in the theater.*

Triremes and ship-sheds: *The naval power of Athens depended on its oared warships, the triremes. Excavations in the harbor at Piraeus have revealed the submerged remains of the ship-sheds which allowed the boats to be stored and maintained out of the water.*

Literacy

One of the earliest examples of Greek writing has been identified on an eighth-century BCE cup found at Pithekoussai, a Greek settlement on an island in the Bay of Naples. The verse inscription records the "cup of Nestor," recalling the mythical Homeric king. Records of public decisions and accounts such as Athens have provided a wealth of detailed information on the running of individual cities.

Colonization

Greek settlements are found around the shores of the Mediterranean and the Black Seas. The name of the modern Spanish city of Ampurias comes from the Greek settlement of Emporion, literally "the trading station." Cities like Corinth were involved with the colonizing movement; one of Sparta's few overseas settlements was at Taras (the modern Taranto) in southern Italy.

The Greeks in Egypt

Although Greeks were not allowed to establish a colony in Egypt, the Greek historian Herodotus recorded the trading settlement of Naukratis in the western Nile Delta. Large quantities of imported Greek pottery have been discovered at the site. Graffiti on offerings placed in the Greek temples of the settlement have helped to identify the ethnic origins of the community, including the city of Miletos in what is now Turkey. Another focal point of the Greek presence in Egypt was the fortress of Daphnae, guarding Egypt's eastern frontier with the Sinai; this is probably to be identified with Tell Defenneh. Pottery finds suggest that the garrison may have been drawn from Ionia (western Turkey and the off-shore Aegean islands.)

Oracle at Delphi

Herodotus also described the role of the oracle at Delphi, one of the most important oracles in the ancient world. Individual cities had their own treasuries built within the sanctuary to store offerings to the gods. The Treasury of the Athenians was said to have been constructed after the defeat of the Persians at the battle of Marathon in 490 BCE. It was decorated with relief panels showing the two Greek heroes Herakles and Theseus. The Greek alliance dedicated a large intertwined bronze snake supporting a cauldron to mark the defeat of the Persians in 479 BCE. The base has been found in excavations, while the snakes were transported to Constantinople (modern Istanbul) in Late Antiquity and placed in the hippodrome.

Athletic events

A series of athletic events open to Greeks were celebrated at four main sanctuaries, three in the Peloponnese (Olympia, Isthmia, and Nemea) and one in central Greece (Delphi.) The Olympic games started in 776 BCE and were then celebrated every four years. A large stadium, 630 feet (192 meters) long, was constructed to the east of the main sanctuary at Olympia. In its third phase it may have been able to hold 43,000 spectators. Victors in the events were commemorated by the dedication of statues; many are listed by the Roman travel-writer Pausanias, and some of the inscribed bases have been found in excavations. During the fifth century BCE a new temple of Zeus was constructed and decorated with sculptures showing the deeds of Herakles. Further three-dimensional sculptures were placed in the triangular pediments at either end of the building. At the east end these depicted the foundation myth of the sanctuary, the chariot race of Oinomaos and Pelops, and at the west end, the great battle between the Lapiths and the Centaurs.

Macedonia and the Hellenistic World

During the fourth century BCE, the kingdom of Macedonia in northern Greece expanded and defeated some of the older Greek states. This allowed Macedonia, under Alexander the Great, to launch an attack on the Persian Empire which took Greek culture to Egypt, Mesopotamia, and as far as the Indus Valley. After Alexander's death in 323 BCE, the new territories were divided into separate kingdoms under dynasties such as the Ptolemies and Seleucids.

The Macedonian phalanx

The Macedonian infantry's strength lay in a military fromation called the phalanx which consisted of a wall of men armed with long pikes. This gave them advantage over the armoured hoplites of other Greek states, reflected in Philip II's great victory at Chaironeia in Boeotia in 338 BCE over the Athenian and Theban alliance.

Pergamon

The Attalid kings constructed a royal city in north-west Anatolia during the third and second centuries BCE. Its position, on the top of a steep mountain, gave it a dramatic setting which was intended to evoke the Athenian acropolis. One of the inspirations for the city was the defeat of the Gauls; this was commemorated in a series of

Timeline

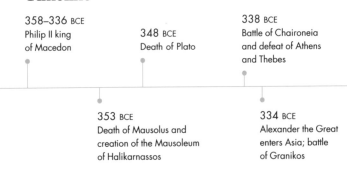

358–336 BCE
Philip II king
of Macedon

348 BCE
Death of Plato

338 BCE
Battle of Chaironeia
and defeat of Athens
and Thebes

353 BCE
Death of Mausolus and
creation of the Mausoleum
of Halikarnassos

334 BCE
Alexander the Great
enters Asia; battle
of Granikos

sculptural groups on the acropolis placed within the sanctuary of Athena. The defeat of the Gauls probably inspired the monumental altar of Zeus, which was decorated with a continuous frieze showing the defeat of the Giants by the Olympian gods.

Alexandria

Alexander the Great acquired Egypt, and his general Ptolemy established a dynasty which lasted until the death of Cleopatra. The royal city of Alexandria was established on the coast of the western Nile Delta. It boasted a library and the celebrated lighthouse. Underwater surveys have revealed remains of the ancient city including numerous sculptures.

The Mausoleum of Halikarnassos

Mausolus was the local Persian official or ruler in Caria, now western Turkey. When he died in 353 BCE, his wife Artemisia erected a monumental tomb at Halikarnassos (the modern Bodrum.) A series of Greek sculptors, such as Skopas and Bryaxis, were commissioned to create this monument. Among the sculptural themes was the Amazonomachy, the mythical battle between the Greeks and Amazons. Free-standing sculptures, perhaps showing members of Mausolus's family, were placed around the building, though their precise positions are not known.

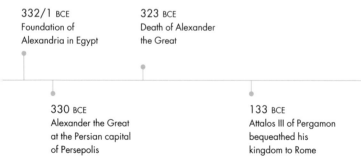

332/1 BCE
Foundation of
Alexandria in Egypt

323 BCE
Death of Alexander
the Great

330 BCE
Alexander the Great
at the Persian capital
of Persepolis

133 BCE
Attalos III of Pergamon
bequeathed his
kingdom to Rome

Italy and the Roman world

A small settlement on the banks of the river Tiber in central Italy was to become one of the largest cities of the ancient world. The city of Rome came to dominate Italy and then expanded into areas, such as Sicily, which had been colonized by the Greeks. Further conflicts brought Macedonia, and then the rest of Greece, into the Roman sphere of influence. By the end of the Roman Republic the empire stretched from the English Channel to North Africa, from Spain to Egypt, and further expansion was to continue under the emperors.

Etruscans

The area of modern Tuscany to the north of Rome contained a series of Etruscan city-states. Extensive rock-cut cemeteries contained thousands of imported pieces of Greek pottery, much of it made in Athens in the sixth and fifth centuries BCE. The tombs themselves were often highly decorated, sometimes with scenes of banqueting. The harbour-town of Pyrgi contained gold plaques which have helped archaeologists to read the Etruscan language.

Italy and Roman world timeline

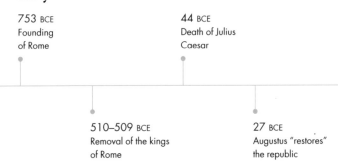

753 BCE
Founding
of Rome

44 BCE
Death of Julius
Caesar

510–509 BCE
Removal of the kings
of Rome

27 BCE
Augustus "restores"
the republic

Roman Corinth

The Hellenistic city of Corinth was destroyed by Rome in 146 BCE and the site lay deserted for nearly 100 years. A Roman colony was established in 44 BCE by Julius Caesar. Inscriptions show that Latin was the main public language of the new city until the early second century CE. The architecture and portraiture were also designed to give the city a Roman rather than Greek feel. The city was served by two of the largest harbors in the ancient world: Cenchreae, which gave access to the eastern Mediterranean, and Lechaeum on the Corinthian Gulf, the route to Italy.

Temples of Mithras

The god Mithras came from the area of Persia. The cult became very popular with Roman soldiers and several temples have been found in Germany and Britain. Mithraism was a mystery cult and there was an elaborate series of initiations. A series of three inscribed altars, dating to the early part of the third century CE, were found in the temple at Carrawburgh, on Hadrian's wall in the UK. Each had been dedicated by the commander of the local Roman garrison.

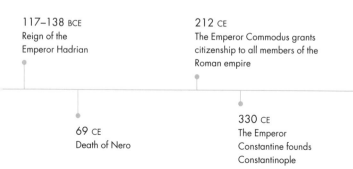

117–138 BCE
Reign of the
Emperor Hadrian

212 CE
The Emperor Commodus grants
citizenship to all members of the
Roman empire

69 CE
Death of Nero

330 CE
The Emperor
Constantine founds
Constantinople

Augustan Rome

Rome's first emperor, Augustus, claimed to have transformed the city. One of his building projects was the construction of a family mausoleum on the banks of the river Tiber, surmounted by a statue of the emperor. Adjacent to it was an elaborate altar of Peace (the Ara Pacis), surrounded by carved marble screens that showed members of the imperial family and the Roman elite. Augustus also transformed the heart of the city with the construction of a new forum.

Vindolanda

A decision was made to destroy the garrison archive of a Roman army unit stationed at Vindolanda, on Rome's northern frontier in Great Britain, when they abandoned the fort for service in Trajan's campaign across the Danube. However, some of the documents – written on wooden tablets – escaped the fire and they provide a significant insight to frontier life in northern Britain. Details include the fighting strength of the unit; many members of the garrison were on secondment elsewhere or ill. There are also glimpses of personal lives, with correspondence between the wives of the garrison commanders.

Northern Frontier

During the reign of the emperor Hadrian (117–138 CE), Rome constructed a permanent frontier in northern England, known as Hadrian's Wall. It stretched for over 70 miles (112 kilometers) between the river Tyne in the east and the Solway Firth in the west. The frontier was extended westwards by a series of watchtowers. The wall was built in several phases; in the western parts it was originally constructed from turf which was later replaced in stone. There were fortlets every mile with two towers in between them. A number of larger forts for both infantry and cavalry units were later built along the line of the wall.

Pompeii

The town of Pompeii was destroyed during the volcanic eruption of Vesuvius on 24 August, 79 CE. This preserved the walls of the buildings allowing a unique glimpse of the decoration in private houses that is virtually unrivaled among surviving evidence of the Roman world. Many buildings had previously been damaged in a major earthquake in 62 CE. During excavations, hollows in the ash were filled with plaster of paris to obtain a cast of the original objects which included human bodies as well as other organic material.

ABOVE The Forum, Pompeii: Tibere's triumphal arch and Macellum portico (covered market.)

Herculaneum

The town of Herculaneum on the slopes of Vesuvius was overwhelmed by a series of pyroclastic flows. A number of bodies found along the sea shore show the force of the destruction. Many wooden features, such as doors and furniture, in the buildings from the 79 CE eruption, were carbonized and thus preserved.

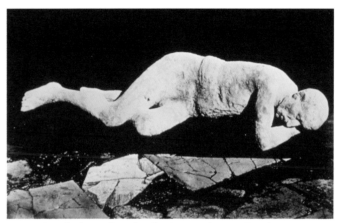

ABOVE Cast of a human figure found in Pompeii, dating to the volcanic eruption of Vesuvius in 79 CE.

Ostia

The massive urban population of Rome required a secure source of food. This was assisted by the development of the major port of Ostia at the mouth of the river Tiber. An enclosed harbor, known as Portus, was constructed by the emperor Claudius just to the north to allow ships to transfer their grain cargoes to warehouses; it was then transferred to barges, which took the supplies 22 miles (35 kilometers) up the river to Rome.

Constantinople

The city of Constantinople – modern Istanbul – was established in 330 CE on the site of the older Greek settlement of Byzantion, on the European side of the Bosporos. The great church of Hagia Sophia was originally constructed in 360. This royal city was embellished with works of art from across the empire. Among them was the bronze serpent monument dedicated by the Hellenic League at Delphi in thanksgiving to Apollo for the defeat of the Persians in 479 BCE.

FACT
Constantine (272–337 CE) was declared emperor in York in 306. He celebrated his victory over Maxentius at the Milvian Bridge in 312 by the creation of a monumental arch in Rome next to the Colosseum, the Arch of Constantine.

Masada

This craggy outcrop on the edge of the Judean desert became the site of one of Herod the Great's most magnificent palaces. A series of platforms provided views northwards towards the Dead Sea and the Jordan Valley. His close links with Rome are reflected in the choice of architecture and painted decoration for the residential parts of this structure. When the Jews revolted against Rome in 66 CE, Masada became a key fortress. Its siege was described in detail by the historian Josephus. Masada was encircled by a wall and a series of forts, with the largest placed directly opposite the royal palace. A massive siege ramp was constructed, which still stands today, its wood preserved in the dryness of the desert. Although Josephus records a mass suicide of the Jewish garrison, little evidence of bodies has been found.

Town life

In the Roman world, towns were centers of administration and of religious, economic, and cultural life. They tended to show signs of regular street planning and were connected by networks of roads and waterways. Typical features included:

Bath-houses: *Roman baths consisted of a series of rooms of varying temperatures, from the* frigidarium *(with cold plunges) to the* caldarium *(sauna). Rome had a series of bathing establishments. Among them were the baths started by the emperor Caracalla – it is estimated that the complex could have met the needs of some 10,000 bathers.*

Aqueducts: *Roman engineering allowed water to be carried to urban centers by long aqueducts. One of the longest was built around 345* CE *to supply the city of Constantinople; it stretched for some 93 miles*

ABOVE A Roman bath house at Aquae Sulis, now called Bath, in the UK.

ABOVE The Colosseum, the giant amphitheater in the center of the city of Rome.

(150 kilometers) bringing water from Thrace. The system was later extended with one line running for 155 miles (250 kilometers.)

Arenas: *After the death of Emperor Nero in 69* CE, *the part of the city covered by his sprawling palace complex became public property. The new emperor, Vespasian (69–79* CE), *used part of this land for the creation of a major amphitheater known as the Colosseum, first used in 80* CE. *This four-storey structure, some 157 feet (48 meters) high, could seat around 50,000 people (though ancient sources hint at an even greater capacity.)*

Roads: *The Roman empire was criss-crossed by a network of roads which were essential for the movement of troops in frontier areas. Distances were marked by milestones often including details of the emperor under whose reign the work was conducted. The Via Appia linked the city of Rome with Brindisi (the ancient Brundisium) on the Adriatic and then gave access to the eastern provinces through the Via Egnatia, which cut across northern Greece and the province of Macedonia.*

Chart of Roman emperors

Date	Emperor	Date	Emperor
27 BCE–14 CE	Augustus	235–238 CE	Maximinus Thrax
14–37 CE	Tiberius	238 CE	Gordian I
37–41CE	Gaius (Caligula)	238 CE	Gordian II
41–54 CE	Claudius	238 CE	Pupienus Maximus
54–68 CE	Nero	238 CE	Balbinus
68–69 CE	Galba	238–244 CE	Gordian III
69 CE	Otho	244–249 CE	Philip the Arab
69 CE	Vitellius	249–251 CE	Decius
69–79 CE	Vespasian	251–253 CE	Trebonianus Gallus
79–81 CE	Titus	251–252 CE	Hostilianus
81–96 CE	Domitian	253 CE	Aemilianus
96–98 CE	Nerva	253–260 CE	Valerianus
98–117 CE	Trajan	253–268 CE	Gallienus
117–138 CE	Hadrian	268–270 CE	Claudius Gothicus
138–161 CE	Antoninus Pius	270–275 CE	Aurelianus
161–180 CE	Marcus Aurelius	275 CE	interregnum
161–169 CE	Lucius Verus (co-regent with Marcus Aurelius)	275–276 CE	Tacitus
		276 CE	Florianus
180–192 CE	Commodus	276–282 CE	Probus
193 CE	Pertinax	282–283 CE	Carus
193 CE	Didius Julianus	283–285 CE	Carinus
193–194 CE	Pescennius Niger	283–284 CE	Numerianus
193–197 CE	Clodius Albinus	284–305 CE	Diocletianus
193–211 CE	Septimius Severus	286–305 CE	Maximianus
198–217 CE	Caracalla (co-regent with his father, Septimius Severus)	292–306 CE	Conatantius Chlorus
211 CE	Geta (co-regent with his father and brother)	293–311 CE	Galerius
		305–313 CE	Maximinus Daia
217–218 CE	Macrinus	305–307 CE	Flavius Severus
217–218 CE	Diadumenian	306–312 CE	Maxentius
218–222 CE	Elagabalus	308–323 CE	Licinius
222–235 CE	Alexander Severus	306–337 CE	Constantine the Great

AUSTRALIA
AND OCEANIA

Early agricultural systems in Melanesia

The ancient history of Australia and Oceania begins with evidence of horticulture in the New Guinea Highlands around 7000 BCE continuing up to the settlement of New Zealand in 1200 CE. Geographically, the area includes Australia and the many lands of Oceania, including New Zealand, New Guinea, and the islands of the Malay Archipelago.

The New Guinea Highlands are an independent center of the development of food production. Evidence for horticulture first appears around 7000 BCE in the form of swamp drainage channels, though it is not known what crops were cultivated. Although there is no evidence for domesticated forms of local animal species, people clearly had close relationships with various animals, and several species (including small wallabies and possums) seem to have been deliberately introduced to the Bismarck Archipelago and the Solomon Islands some time before 6000 BCE.

By 1500 BCE, there is increasing evidence in the Highlands for forest clearance, soil erosion, and complex field systems, thought to be for growing taro, sugarcane, and bananas. In the lowlands,

Timeline

7000 BCE
First evidence of horticulture in New Guinea Highlands

4000 BCE onwards
Innovations in tool types in Australia, evidence for exploitation of new resources

tree crops such as canarium, coconut, pandanus, and possibly sago were also cultivated. Domestic pigs were probably introduced about 1500 BCE and rapidly became a key source of wealth in New Guinea societies. The introduction of the sweet potato from America about 400 years ago led to intensification of food production, especially in the Highlands.

Pacific colonization

The Pacific was the last area of the globe to be colonized by humans and this could only have been achieved with a high level of seafaring skills.

Lapita complex

About 1500 BCE, the Lapita cultural complex first appeared in the Western Pacific, characterized by distinctive pottery styles, shell artifacts, stone adzes, obsidian artifacts, and an economy based on fish and shellfish, and domesticated plants and animals. Lapita settlements are found as far east as Fiji and Samoa and seem to have been linked by long-distance trade. Lapita is believed to be linked to the spread of speakers of Austronesian languages into the Pacific.

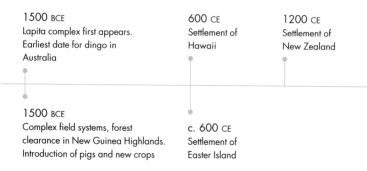

1500 BCE
Lapita complex first appears.
Earliest date for dingo in
Australia

600 CE
Settlement of
Hawaii

1200 CE
Settlement of
New Zealand

1500 BCE
Complex field systems, forest
clearance in New Guinea Highlands.
Introduction of pigs and new crops

c. 600 CE
Settlement of
Easter Island

Settlement of Polynesia

Lapita settlers were well established in Western Polynesia by 100 BCE. Perhaps as a result of population growth and food shortages, people began to colonize the remainder of the Polynesian triangle from about 500 CE. Within a few hundred years, they had reached Hawaii, Easter Island, and finally New Zealand.

Hunting and gathering communities of Australia

Australia was the only land mass to be exclusively occupied by hunting and gathering communities until European colonisation in the late eighteenth century. Beginning about 4000 BCE there is increasing evidence of innovation in technology and management of food resources. The dingo was introduced about 4,000 years ago.

Resource management in Australia: fisheries and firestick farming

Large complexes of stone weirs, traps, holding ponds and channels at Lake Condah and elsewhere in southwest Victoria provide evidence of intensive eel aquaculture. The reliable food supplies allowed people to hold large ceremonial gatherings, sometimes lasting several months. The precise age of the site is unknown, but it is thought to be at least 4000 years old.

Easter Island

A remote speck in the South Pacific, Easter Island, or "Rapa Nui," was settled by people from eastern Polynesia, probably in the mid-first millennium CE. On Easter Sunday (April 5) 1722, Dutch navigators encountered the island, and gave it its current name. The Polynesian colonists had radically changed the landscape by clearing the palm forest to plant their crops and to obtain timber.

They constructed *ahu* (stone platforms) from cores of rubble encased with often well-cut stone slabs, and more than 800 *moai* (stone statues) were carved, nearly all of them in soft, volcanic tuff. All the statues were variations on a theme, a human figure with a prominent, angular nose and chin, and often elongated perforated ears containing disks. The bodies, which end at the abdomen, have arms held tightly to the sides, and hands held in front, with long fingertips meeting a stylized loincloth. They are believed to represent ancestor figures.

The final phase of the island's prehistory saw the collapse of the earlier way of life: statues ceased to be carved, and 1,000 years of peaceful coexistence were shattered, as shown by the manufacture of *mataa*, spearheads and daggers of obsidian, in huge quantities. Conflicts led to the toppling of all the statues, and a new social system arose where an annual leader or "birdman" was chosen by competition.

ABOVE Moai statues on Easter Island in the South Pacific Ocean.

FACT

The statues range from 6.5–32 feet (2–10 meters) in height, and weigh up to 82 tons (74 tonnes). "El Gigante," the biggest statue carved, was never finished. It is over 65 feet (20 meters) high and probably weighs 270 tons (244 tonnes).

Nan Madol

Sometimes known as the "Venice of the Pacific," the massive platforms of the ceremonial complex at Nan Madol on Ponape in the Caroline Islands rise out of the waters of a tidal lagoon. Begun about 1000 CE, Nan Madol flourished for a few centuries during which a single dynasty united the chiefdoms of Ponape.

ABOVE Nan Madol is the greatest record of prehistoric achievement in Micronesia.

NORTH AMERICA

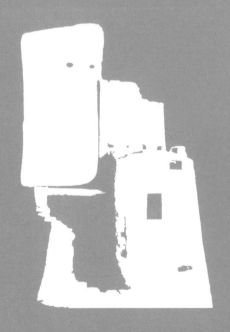

Developing societies

After millennia of leading a nomadic, hunter-gatherer existence, Ancient North Americans developed a number of complex societies whose traces are still highly visible today. In the East and Midwest they built mounds, some of the designs and functions of which remain a mystery today. In the south-west, dramatic cliff-dwellings were constructed to house huge populations, like modern apartment blocks. The nature of Native American life changed dramatically once it came into contact with Europeans.

Paleo-Indian and archaic North America (up to 1000 BCE)

While the exact chronology of human intrusion into North America continues to be debated, it is generally believed that people from Asia came into the country at least 13,000 years ago, on foot across the frozen Bering strait and in boats down the Pacific coast. For the first millennia of occupation, native North Americans' primary subsistence patterns were non-agricultural and mobile. People lived hunter-gatherer lifestyles, exploiting wild plants and hunting and fishing for game. By 3000 BCE, people had begun to settle more permanently and squash, sunflower, and several other native plants

Timeline

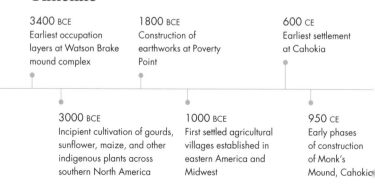

3400 BCE
Earliest occupation layers at Watson Brake mound complex

1800 BCE
Construction of earthworks at Poverty Point

600 CE
Earliest settlement at Cahokia

3000 BCE
Incipient cultivation of gourds, sunflower, maize, and other indigenous plants across southern North America

1000 BCE
First settled agricultural villages established in eastern America and Midwest

950 CE
Early phases of construction of Monk's Mound, Cahokia

were in the process of being domesticated. Around 1000 BCE populations in certain areas had become primarily or entirely sedentary, dependent on incipient agriculture and developing long-distance trading routes for exotic goods.

Buffalo Jumps

The remains of buffalo jumps are found throughout the grasslands of the northern plains of North America, in US states and Canadian provinces such as Montana, Wyoming, and Alberta. For thousands of years, Plains Indians killed bison by driving them in controlled stampedes over cliffs, until the virtual extinction of the bison caused by European Americans in the nineteenth century. They directed the buffalo along "drive lanes," made of stone cairns, to the drop-off point. Hundreds of animals could be killed in a single drive; bone beds up to 40 feet (12 meters) in depth have been found at the bottom of the cliffs.

The Woodland period mound builders
(1000 BCE–1000 CE)

The tradition of mound building in eastern North America began in the second millennium BCE. It was continued for over 2,000 years by people whom archaeologists call the Adena culture (1000–100 BCE) and Hopewell complex (200 BCE–500 CE.) The mounds take a

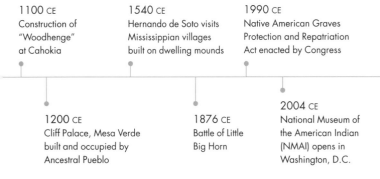

1100 CE
Construction of "Woodhenge" at Cahokia

1540 CE
Hernando de Soto visits Mississippian villages built on dwelling mounds

1990 CE
Native American Graves Protection and Repatriation Act enacted by Congress

1200 CE
Cliff Palace, Mesa Verde built and occupied by Ancestral Pueblo

1876 CE
Battle of Little Big Horn

2004 CE
National Museum of the American Indian (NMAI) opens in Washington, D.C.

variety of forms and their use varies over time and region. There are effigy mounds, earthen burial mounds of different shapes and sizes, and also platform mounds, all once common throughout the American Midwest. Other earthen constructions of this period include circular- or square-ditched enclosures and hilltop enclosures.

Mounded communities *Certain mound groups were probably occupation areas. Poverty Point is one of the best known – and one of the oldest – of these mounded communities. It was constructed and occupied between 1500 and 400 BCE and consists of six large semi-circular ridges and several platform and effigy mounds.*

Conical grave mounds *These were often grouped into cemeteries built over the remains of large wooden enclosures, and there is evidence of long periods of use and rebuilding. These mounds often contain multiple burials and exotic artifacts such as pearl beads, perforated bear teeth, textiles, copper ornaments, and carved mica. Some of these mounds have flat surfaces which may have been used as platforms for ritual activities.*

Effigy mounds *Many earthworks in the Mississippi valley seem to have been built as effigy mounds in the shape of animals. The best example is Great Serpent Mound, in southern Ohio, in the form of a snake holding an egg in its mouth. The mound is made of earth heaped on a base of clay and stone. It was originally thought to date to the early Woodland Adena culture (1000–100 BCE), but it is possible that the mound is much later, perhaps dating to the Mississippian Culture, around 1,000 years ago. Archaeologists have found it impossible to determine what the effigy mound signified in its builders' ideology.*

FACT
Watson Brake is an oval of 11 mounds connected by a low ridge. It is the oldest mound site in North America, having recently been radiocarbon dated to 3400 BCE, well before any other sites known in North America.

The Mississippian period
(700–1500 CE)

After 500 BCE, farming of maize and other native plants became common, and people all along the Mississippi valley began to settle in permanent villages. Some of these communities developed complex social and political hierarchies. People constructed enormous multi-tiered mounds on which they built their houses. Typically, the higher one lived on the mound, the higher one's social status.

Cahokia

The most famous, and largest, of these mound-cities is Cahokia, located just east of St. Louis. As many as 20,000 people may have lived there at its peak, around 1200 CE. Its inhabitants relied on the cultivation of maize and other plants, and engaged in long-distance trade across a large part of the continent. The most spectacular feature of the whole complex is Monk's Mound, a rectangular, multi-storey earthen mound. On top of the mound was a chieftain's or religious structure. Close to Monk's Mound is "Woodhenge," a circular post structure that served as a calendar oriented to the rising sun. Only the postholes remain from the original structure.

People of the south-western deserts
(0–1500 CE)

The dry deserts of Arizona, New Mexico, and adjacent southern Utah and Colorado have been occupied by mobile foragers for at least 10.000 years. About 2,500 years ago, some groups turned to the cultivation of maize, beans, and squash and the result was some of the most spectacular archaeological cultures in North America. Archaeologists have organized the archaeological sites and material culture of the Southwest into three major regional traditions: the Anasazi tradition (now called Ancestral Pueblo) is found in the Four Corners region, where the states of Arizona, Colorado, New Mexico, and Utah meet; the Mogollon in central Arizona and the adjacent part of New Mexico; and the Hohokam in Central Arizona.

Regional traditions

The Ancestral Pueblo populations (700–1500 CE) flourished in the high deserts of the Colorado Plateau. They were agriculturalists and traders who lived in cliff dwellings, such as the famous ones at Mesa Verde National Park in southern Colorado, and traveled along the arrow-straight roads they built between these settlements.

The Mogollon tradition (200–1400 CE) is best known for its beautifully-decorated pottery. These people lived in Ancestral Pueblo-style dwellings and buried their dead with elegant, thin-walled vessels (called Mimbres pottery) decorated with geometric designs and stylized humans and animals.

In the Sonoran Desert, Hohokam people (200–1500 CE) may have acted as middlemen for trade between northern Mexico, the California Coast, the Rocky Mountains, and the Great Plains. They built extensive irrigation networks with massive canals – some several miles long and over 65 feet (20 meters) across.

Mesa Verde cliff dwellings

The flat-topped mesas of the region were first occupied about 10,000 years ago by early hunters and gatherers. The sites that bring millions of tourists to the area are much later, dating to around

ABOVE Cliff Palace, the cliff dwellings at Mesa Verde, c. 600–1300 CE.

600–1300 CE. The most photographed of these are the multi-storey, multi-room villages (or pueblos) built in large alcoves in the walls of the canyons that dissect the mesas. The structures were made from sandstone, mortar, and wood. The walls of the houses were lined with plaster and very often still retain the remains of the multi-colored paintings that originally adorned them. Cliff Palace contains over 200 individual rooms and *kivas*, circular, stone-lined subterranean chambers. Even today these chambers are important in the religious, social, and ceremonial life of the Pueblo Indians, the descendants of the Anasazi or Ancestral Pueblo populations who built these sites. These cliff dwellings were occupied for only 75 to 100 years, before the mesas were abandoned at the end of the thirteenth century, perhaps because of drought.

European contact
(1000 CE–PRESENT)

Archaeology has revealed that North America was contacted by Europeans long before Christopher Columbus in 1492. The site of L'Anse aux Meadows, on the coast of Newfoundland, is the best evidence for Viking settlement of North America. Excavations have revealed the remains of eight houses, several smaller buildings, a smithy, and a charcoal kiln, as well as various Viking objects from the eleventh century CE. The site was occupied for only about 30 years before being abandoned, either because the climate was too harsh for agriculturalists or simply because of its extreme isolation. L'Anse aux Meadows may have been one of the colonies established by Erik the Red after he was banished from Norway in 982 CE.

North American archaeology reveals that the period of contact with Europeans is distinctly different from that which preceded it. Much of this study is focused on marginalized people and communities like prostitutes, slaves, Native Americans, and political activists. It has illuminated the history of conflicts between Native Americans and white settlers and it has revealed traces of many of the less well-known aspects of pioneer and United States history.

Little Bighorn

On June 25, 1876, General George Armstrong Custer and 647 men of the 7th Cavalry rode into a huge Indian village with as many as 7,000 inhabitants, along the Little Bighorn River. Custer's mission was to coerce Cheyenne Indians back onto their reservation in South Dakota. Custer's immediate command, comprising 210 cavalrymen, were all killed. Only about 60 Indians died. Although the basic chronology of the battle is known, it has been difficult to piece together many other important events of that fateful day; little specific information was recovered from the Indians, who departed immediately after the battle, and none of Custer's command survived. Between 1983 and 1996, a team from the National Park Service conducted archaeological investigations at the site and the surrounding area. They were able to identify items like spent bullets and iron arrowheads. The National Park Service also analyzed the skeletal remains of some of the cavalrymen who were killed, often with gruesome results; forensic analysis of the skeletal remains revealed that one cavalryman had been shot in the chest and then in the head. His skull was smashed in, and his body shot with arrows and slashed with knives.

ABOVE War cemetery at Little Bighorn, the site of Custer's Last Stand.

MESOAMERICA

Early societies

Mesoamerica, or Middle America, is a culturally and economically integrated area composed of diverse ethnic groups, such as the Maya, Aztec, Zapotec, and Mixtec. It is so-identified because of its geographic position between North and South America; it extends from the northern Mexican deserts to eastern Honduras and El Salvador. Mesoamericans were agriculturalists, relying principally on maize and secondarily on beans and squash. They were organized into stratified societies, although they lacked metal tools and pack animals throughout their history. Mesoamerican cities were noted for their monumental stone architecture, including ballcourts, and stone sculpture, and for their specialists who produced hieroglyphic books to record a complex calendar.

Significant changes began after 5000 BCE, when the introduction of maize agriculture oriented people toward a village way of life. Social stratification became marked with the rise of the Mokaya chiefdoms of coastal Chiapas, Mexico, beginning around 1600 BCE. Pottery first appeared around this time as well, significantly later than in either North or South America.

Timeline

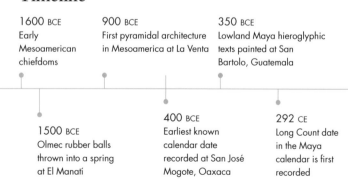

1600 BCE
Early Mesoamerican chiefdoms

900 BCE
First pyramidal architecture in Mesoamerica at La Venta

350 BCE
Lowland Maya hieroglyphic texts painted at San Bartolo, Guatemala

1500 BCE
Olmec rubber balls thrown into a spring at El Manatí

400 BCE
Earliest known calendar date recorded at San José Mogote, Oaxaca

292 CE
Long Count date in the Maya calendar is first recorded

The Olmec (1200–400 BCE)

The Olmec, Mesoamerica's first civilization, emerged around 1200 BCE, with the rise of San Lorenzo, Veracruz, a center of artistic and architectural innovation that served a highly centralized political system. Many basic patterns of Mesoamerican religion and material culture, such as a belief in a multi-layered, four-directional universe, and the ritual use of jade and rubber, first become apparent at this time. The San Lorenzo Olmec forged ties with far-flung groups, such as those in the central Mexican highlands, contributing greatly to the unified character of Mesoamerica.

The intensification of Olmec influence (900–400 BCE)

The Middle Preclassic period in Mesoamerica witnessed the rise of La Venta, Tabasco, and the demise of San Lorenzo. This was the most fertile period of Olmec influence, laying the foundation for the political organization, art styles, and hieroglyphic writing systems that followed, including the famous Lowland Maya.

Symbolization became quite sophisticated as well, and seems to have led to a nascent writing system. Stimulus from Middle Preclassic Olmec contact led to the development of chiefdoms throughout Mesoamerica. These deployed comparable symbols of political power, such as large mounds and platforms, stone sculpture, and carved jade.

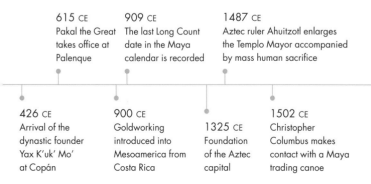

615 CE
Pakal the Great takes office at Palenque

909 CE
The last Long Count date in the Maya calendar is recorded

1487 CE
Aztec ruler Ahuitzotl enlarges the Templo Mayor accompanied by mass human sacrifice

426 CE
Arrival of the dynastic founder Yax K'uk' Mo' at Copán

900 CE
Goldworking introduced into Mesoamerica from Costa Rica

1325 CE
Foundation of the Aztec capital

1502 CE
Christopher Columbus makes contact with a Maya trading canoe

Late Preclassic regional developments
(400 BCE–200 CE)

Regional states and chiefdoms with distinctly local flavors developed in the Late Preclassic period, shown by large ceremonial centers of the Zapotec of Oaxaca, such as San José Mogote and Monte Albán. While concerns with warfare are muted in Olmec art, they dominate Zapotec art, suggesting greater emphasis on internecine warfare. Zapotec sites preserve the earliest record of the 260-day divinatory calendar used in most Mesoamerican societies.

The Izapan culture was directly influenced by the Olmec. It flourished on the Pacific coast and piedmont of Chiapas and Guatemala during the Late Preclassic. Izapans are thought to have influenced the development of Lowland Maya civilization, which still shows no evidence of direct Olmec contact. Political centralization of the Maya Lowlands progressed rapidly during the Late Preclassic with El Mirador, Guatemala, emerging as the dominant center. Narrative painting, complex symbolism, and hieroglyphic texts, for which the ancient Maya are so famous, were already well-developed, as witnessed by murals at San Bartolo, Guatemala, dating from before 150 BCE.

Classic Mesoamerica 100–900 CE

A key event in the Classic period was the emergence of the city of Teotihuacán, Mexico, 25 miles (40 kilometers) northeast of Mexico City. Its name and those of its famous buildings derive from Aztec (Nahuatl) terms, although we do not know what language was spoken at Teotihuacán. A demographic and political transformation in central Mexico occurred around the turn of the millennium, when the population dramatically expanded at Teotihuacán. By 100 CE major building projects were under way, including the massive Pyramids of the Sun and Moon, and, around 200 CE, the Ciudadela and Temple of the Feathered Serpent. The city was laid out in an exacting grid-plan with 2,000 residential apartment compounds flanking the ceremonial core. Teotihuacán had an ambitious agenda

Chart of Reigns of Some Notable Maya Kings

Maya Kings	Dates	Maya Kings	Dates
Chak Tok Ich'aak I (Tikal)	360–378	Bird Jaguar IV	752–768
Siyah Chan K'awiil II	411–456	Ruler 4 (Piedras Negras)	729–757
Jasaw Chan K'awiil I-	682–734	K'inich Janaab Pakal I (Palenque)	615–683
Yuknoom Ch'een II (Calakmul)	636–695	K'inich Ahkal Mo' Naab III	721–736
Yuknoom Yich'aak K'ak'	686–695	K'inich Yax K'uk' Mo' (Copán)	426–437
K'ak' Tiliw Chan (Naranjo)	693–728	Waxaklajuun Ubaah K'awiil	695–738
Itzamnaaj Balam II (Yaxchilan)	681–742	Yax Pasaj Chan Yoaat	763–?

of economic expansion and political domination founded on control of the obsidian trade. The city was violently destroyed around 650 CE.

The Classic Maya (250-900 CE)

Teotihuacán influence infiltrated every culture in Mesoamerica during the Classic era. Political organization was highly centralized, with authority vested in a single semi-divine figure, a *k'uhulajaw* or "holy lord," whose wealth rested on an economy of redistribution and tribute. Teotihuacán influence on this political system, and its attendant art, largely related to the ideology and trappings of warfare.

Though the Classic Lowland Maya flourished, the region was never unified but rather fragmented into hundreds of autonomous polities. This divisive but artistically brilliant era lasted until about 800 CE, when conditions deteriorated possibly due to destructive warfare exacerbated by drought conditions.

FACT

Archaeologist Saburo Sugiyama discovered the skeletons of 200 males dressed as warriors, buried under the Temple of the Feathered Serpent as part of the building's dedication.

Mesoamerican writing

Mesoamerica had the only advanced writing systems in the Precolumbian New World. The Zapotec and Isthmian scripts probably represent true writing; however, only Lowland Maya writing expressed nuanced spoken language and is well understood today. Numerical bars (equaling five) and dots (equaling one) were used for calendrical record-keeping which also entailed a vegisimal place-notation system and the use of zero.

The Postclassic world (1000–1521 CE)

The power vacuum left by the fall of Teotihuacán in the seventh century laid the groundwork for Postclassic Mesoamerica. Militant states arose in central Mexico in the eighth century and used Teotihuacán art as the basis of a new visual vocabulary of power featuring the Feathered Serpent. The most famous of these is Tula Hidalgo, home of the enigmatic Toltec. This period also saw extensive southerly migrations of Nahua-speaking people who wandered as far as Nicaragua. Central-Mexican cultural influence dominated the Terminal Classic/Postclassic period, seen, for instance, at Chichén Itzá, a Maya city replete with "Toltec" art and architecture, and also at El Tajin, the largest polity of Terminal Classic Veracruz.

BELOW Chac Mool, a type of Mesoamerican stone altar, from Cancun, Mexico.

FACT

In 1978 electrical workers in downtown Mexico City unearthed a relief sculpture depicting the dismembered body of the sister of the Aztec's patron god Huitzilopochtli. The discovery of the Coyolxauhqui Stone led to the more impressive find of the Templo Mayor, or Great Temple.

The Aztecs

The Postclassic period culminated in the rise of the Aztecs, or more narrowly the Mexica, whose origins lie somewhere on the northern "Chichimec" fringe of Mesoamerica. They migrated into the Valley of Mexico at the end of the Classic period, like other Nahuatl-speaking groups, and settled around Lake Texcoco. Through political intrigue and steely determination, the Aztecs eventually established a capital city at Tenochtitlán, present day Mexico City. By forging ties with Tetzcoco and Tlacopan, called the Triple Alliance, the Aztecs were able to subjugate local populations and more far-flung peoples, such as the Huastec, Mixtec, Totonac, and Zoque, all of whom provided tribute, such as cacao, rubber, textiles, and finely wrought crafts. While they were poised at the edge of the Maya world, any plans for future conquest were dashed by the arrival of the Spansih under Cortés in 1519, leading to their eventual downfall in 1521.

Aztec rulers acceding before European contact

Aztec Rulers	Dates	Aztec Rulers	Dates
Acamapichtli	1375–1395	Axayacatl	1469–1481
Huitzilhuitl	1396–1417	Tizoc-	1481–1486
Chimalpopoca	1417–1426	Ahuitzotl	1486–1502
Itzcoatl	1427–1440	Motecuhzoma II	1502–1520
Motecuhzoma I	1440–1469		

What the Spanish saw in Tenochtitlán

Conquistadors found Tenochtitlán's gleaming pyramids and buildings as astonishing as a vision from a fairy tale, and compared the city in size and grandeur to Constantinople. The Spanish saw vendors in the orderly market selling all manner of items, and wandering officials enforcing legitimate weights and measures and collecting taxes. The market was, in fact, in Tenochtitlán's sister city, Tlateloco, and is believed to have been attended by 60,000 people daily. Cortés was personally escorted by Motecuhzoma I to the top of the main temple, where he saw "idols" smeared with sacrificial blood.

FACT
Cacao beans not only produced chocolate drinks consumed by the Mesoamerican elite but were also used as currency in Aztec times.

ABOVE Cacao beans were central to Mesoamerican civilizations.

SOUTH
AMERICA

Cultural diversity

Native American cultures were a diverse mosaic in Ancient South America, varying from mobile hunting and gathering populations to large, densely populated villages. Large-scale, centralized polities, such as the Inca Empire, developed in the central Andes.

The central Andes

The central Andes were colonized around 13,000 years ago by hunting and gathering peoples. Even at this early phase, there is evidence for interaction between the coast and highlands. For example, obsidian has been found at the site of Quebrada Jaguay that came from a source more than 80 miles (130 kilometers) away.

First mummies

Little is known about the ritual or social life of these early cultures. However, it appears that by 6,000 years ago there was an increased concern with the dead; at Chinchorro, in coastal Chile, the dead were mummified through a process in which the body was stripped of its flesh and the internal organs were removed. The body was then reassembled with reeds and the face modeled with clay. These are the world's oldest known mummies.

Timeline

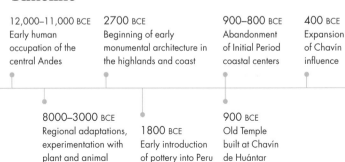

12,000–11,000 BCE
Early human occupation of the central Andes

2700 BCE
Beginning of early monumental architecture in the highlands and coast

900–800 BCE
Abandonment of Initial Period coastal centers

400 BCE
Expansion of Chavín influence

8000–3000 BCE
Regional adaptations, experimentation with plant and animal domestication

1800 BCE
Early introduction of pottery into Peru

900 BCE
Old Temple built at Chavín de Huántar

The Late Preceramic Period (2800–1800 BCE)

Some of the earliest monumental architecture in the New World developed before the appearance of pottery. El Paraíso, located near the city of Lima in Peru, is composed of at least eight stone buildings, some of which are as large as 984 by 328 feet (300 by 100 meters.) To the north, in the Supe and neighboring valleys, archaeologists have located large sites dating to the Late Preceramic period, such as Aspero and Caral. Caral consists of six large platform mounds, several smaller platforms, and two sunken circular plazas.

Religious temples

Religious temples were constructed in the highlands, and include centers such as Huaricoto and Kotosh. Buildings were typically square or rectangular masonry rooms with split-level plaster floors and a central hearth that was the focus of religious offerings. The most famous of these temples is at the site of Kotosh where archaeologists found a large square room containing a clay frieze of crossed human arms.

The Initial Period (1800–800 BCE)

The Initial Period is marked by the first appearance of pottery in Peru, the intensification of an agricultural economy based on irrigation, and other developments such as incipient metallurgy.

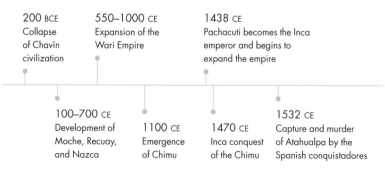

200 BCE
Collapse of Chavín civilization

550–1000 CE
Expansion of the Wari Empire

1438 CE
Pachacuti becomes the Inca emperor and begins to expand the empire

100–700 CE
Development of Moche, Recuay, and Nazca

1100 CE
Emergence of Chimu

1470 CE
Inca conquest of the Chimu

1532 CE
Capture and murder of Atahualpa by the Spanish conquistadores

Most impressive are the monumental temples on the central and northern coasts and highlands. The scale of monumental architecture was much greater here than during the Late Preceramic Period.

Centers such as Garagay and Caballo Muerto had large, life-sized mud friezes depicting anthropomorphic deities. Cerro Sechín in the Casma Valley has a megalithic wall with stone friezes of a procession of warriors, combined with depictions of dismembered body parts. Monuments also appear in the northern highlands region of Peru. Typically they are smaller terraced platforms and include sites such as Pacopampa, Layzón, and Huacaloma.

The Early Horizon (800–200 BCE)

Around 800 BCE many of the large coastal centers of the Initial Period were abandoned. Yet highland sites continued to thrive during the Early Horizon. It was during this time that the site of Chavín de Huántar was established in the north central highlands.

Chavín de Huántar

By about 400 BCE Chavín de Huántar was at least 100 acres (42 hectares) in size, with a residential population of around 3,000. The architectural layout was inspired by Initial Period centers from the coast, but it has unique features, including an elaborate network of narrow passageways known as galleries. It is also known for its complex stone sculpture, depicting religious figures and shamanic religious ideology. Other prominent centers include Kuntur Wasi in the northern highlands, which has recently revealed elaborate elite burials containing gold ornaments with Chavín iconography.

The Early Intermediate Period (200 BCE–500 CE)

Moche culture, from the Early Intermediate Period, is famous for its pottery style: elaborate fine-lined painting, demonstrating religious or mythical events, and modeled pottery showing scenes of everyday life, religious themes, and even graphic sexual content. One of the main Moche capitals was the site of Cerro Blanco, in the Moche

Valley. There are two large platform mounds, Huaca de la Luna and Huaca del Sol, and between these was a complex of residences and workshops that could suggest the presence of Moche urbanism. Recent excavations at Huaca de la Luna have revealed a number of beautiful polychrome murals depicting local deities and processions of prisoners. Moche elites were interred in elaborate graves such as the famous royal tomb found at Sípan, widely regarded as the richest unlooted tomb in the western hemisphere.

Nazca society

Nazca society developed along the south coast of Peru. Nazca is best known for the Nazca Lines, a complex of large geoglyphs depicting geometric shapes, and animals such as monkeys and birds. These figures were drawn on the desert by removing dark rocks in order to expose the underlying light-colored soil. While the exact motivation for their construction has been debated, it is probable that they have ritual associations.

ABOVE Nazca Spider, on the Pampa Colorada.

The Late Intermediate Period (1000–1430 CE)

There was considerable regional diversity in the Late Intermediate Period. In the highlands this period was characterized mainly by the presence of several small-scale polities. On the north coast of Peru, the region was dominated by the Lambayeque and Chimu cultures.

Lambayeque sites, found in the Lambayeque Valley on the north coast of Peru, had large truncated pyramid mounds such as the 12 found at Sican. Chimu sites are found between the Casma Valley and the Motupe Valley. The capital of the Chimu, Chan Chan, was located in the Moche Valley and is best known for 10 adobe enclosures with high walls that served as the palaces for Chimu rulers. Surrounding these enclosures were smaller-scale households and workshops.

The Inca Empire (1438–1532 CE)

The term Inca refers to a specific ethnic group indigenous to the Cuzco region of southern Peru. However, during the fifteenth and sixteenth centuries the Inca expanded to become one of the world's largest empires with Cuzco as its capital.

The Inca Empire covered an immense region, which included the areas we now know as Ecuador, Peru, Chile, western Bolivia, and north-western Argentina. Much of the Inca expansion has been attributed to leader Pachacuti Inca, who expanded the Inca territory significantly beginning around 1438 CE.

Inca expansion and administration was accomplished through a combination of economic and political alliances as well as military conquest. The Inca Empire was divided into provinces, each controlled by administrative centers such as Vilcashuaman, Huanuco Pampa, and Tambo Colorado. The Inca Empire came to an end in 1532 CE, when Pizarro and a company of Spanish soldiers murdered the Inca emperor Atahualpa and eventually descended upon and conquered Cuzco.

LEFT Machu Picchu, Pachacuti Inca's winter palace, Peru.

Bibliography

Chapter 1

McQueen, J. G. 1986. *The Hittites and their Contemporaries in Asia Minor.* Thames & Hudson: London.

Oppenheim, A. L. 1974. *Ancient Mesopotamia: Portrait of a Dead Civilization.* University of Chicago Press: Chicago.

Chapter 2

Snape, S. R. 1997. *Decoding the Stones.* Weidenfeld & Nicolson: London.

Romer, J. 1981. *Valley of the Kings.* Michael O'Mara Books: London.

Chapter 3

McIntosh, Jane. In press (2007). *The Ancient Indus Valley. New Perspectives.* Santa Barbara: ABC-Clio.

Thapar, R. 2003. *The Penguin History of Early India: From the Origins to AD 1300.* London: Penguin.

Chapter 4

Rawson, J. 1996. *Mysteries of Ancient China. New Discoveries from Early Dynasties.* Exhibition catalogue. London: British Museum Press.

Xiaoneng Yang (ed.) 2004. *New Perspectives on China's Past: Twentieth-Century Chinese Archaeology.* Yale: Yale University Press.

Chapter 5

Coulson, D. & Campbell, A. 2001. *African Rock Art: Paintings and Engravings on Stone.* New York: Harry Abrams.

Connah, G. 2001. *African civilisations: An Archaeological Perspective.* Cambridge: Cambridge University Press.

Chapter 6

Cullen, T. Editor. 2001. *Aegean Prehistory: A Review.* American Journal of Archaeology supplement, vol. 1. Boston: Archaeological Institute of America.

Chapter 7

Bogucki, P. I. & P. J. Crabtree 2004. *Ancient Europe 8000 BC–AD 1000: An Encyclopedia of the Barbarian World.* New York: Charles Scribner's Sons.

Castleden, R. 1990. *The Stonehenge People. An Exploration of Life in Neolithic Britain, 4700–2000 BC.* London/New York: Routledge.

Chapter 8

Beard, M., and J. Henderson. 2001. *Classical Art: from Greece to Rome.* Oxford History of Art. Oxford: Oxford University Press.

Shipley, G., J. Vanderspoel, D. Mattingly, and L. Foxhall. Editors. 2006. *The Cambridge Dictionary of Classical Civilization.* Cambridge: Cambridge University Press.

Chapter 9

Mulvaney, J. & J. Kamminga 1999. *Prehistory of Australia.* Allen and Unwin: Sydney.

Flenley, J. & Bahn, P. 2003. *The Enigmas of Easter Island. Island on the Edge.* Oxford University Press: Oxford.

Chapter 10

Milner, G. 2004. *The Moundbuilders: Ancient Peoples of Eastern North Americas.* Thames and Hudson: London.

Thomas, D. H. 1999. *Exploring Ancient Native America. An Archaeological Guide.* Routledge: London

Chapter 11

Coe, M. & R. Koontz 2002. *Mexico: From the Olmecs to the Aztecs.* Thames and Hudson, London.

Sharer, R. 2006. *The Ancient Maya.* Stanford University Press, Stanford.

Smith, M. E. 1996. *The Aztecs.* Blackwell Pub., Oxford, UK.

Chapter 12

Burger, R.L. 1992. *Chavín and the Origins of Andean Civilization.* Thames and Hudson, London.

Moseley, M.E. 2001. *The Incas and their Ancestors: The Archaeology of Peru.* Thames and Hudson, London.

Index

Picture Credits

The publishers would like to thank the following for permission to reproduce images.

Ancient Art and Architecture Collection: p. 8;
David Gill: p. 77;
Getty Images: pp. 30, 34, 43, 83, 117, 132, 134;
iStockphoto: pp. 10, 17, 27, 53, 54, 79;
Joyce Tyldesley: p. 36;
Paul Bahn: pp. 46, 57, 65, 69, 71, 73, 87, 124, 139, 140;
Peter Bogucki: p. 94;
Photolibrary: pp. 84, 108, 111;
Topfoto: pp. 107, 110, 126;
Werner Forman Archive: p. 91

Nomadic hunters

Adena/Hopewell cultures

Marksville culture

Teotihuacán
Monte Albán

San Agustin
Guangala
Moche
Huari
Nazca

Marajo

ATLANTIC OCEAN

ATLANTIC OCEAN

Celts

G
Pe

Roman

Rom

Carthage
Mauretania M.